THE
BEAN
COOKBOOK

BEANS | LENTILS | PEAS | CHICKPEAS

Publisher Mike Sanders
Designer William Thomas
Editor Alexandra Andrzejewski
Art Director Nigel Wright
Food Stylist Tami Hardeman
Photographer Helene Dujardin
Recipe Tester Carolyn Doyle
Proofreader Polly Zetterberg
Indexer Brad Herriman

First American Edition, 2021
Published in the United States by DK Publishing
1450 Broadway, Suite 801, New York, NY 10018

Copyright © 2021 Dorling Kindersley Limited
DK, a Division of Penguin Random House LLC
21 22 23 24 25 10 9 8 7 6 5 4 3 2 1
001-322085-May2021

ISBN 978-0-7440-3460-8

A catalog record for this book
is available from the Library of Congress.

DK books are available at special discounts when purchased
in bulk for sales promotions, premiums, fund-raising, or
educational use. For details, contact:
SpecialSales@dk.com

Printed and bound in China

Reprinted from *Pulse Revolution*

For the curious
www.dk.com

THE
BEAN
COOKBOOK

BEANS | LENTILS | PEAS | CHICKPEAS

*Creative recipes for
every meal of the day*

TAMI HARDEMAN

CONTENTS

INTRODUCTION

HEALTHY & SUSTAINABLE

Beans, lentils, peas, and chickpeas (collectively called pulses) are a nutritious, sustainable, and an integral part of many cuisines. Not only do they taste delicious, but they're also a smart choice for both your body and the world.

PULSES: A KITCHEN STAPLE

Beans, lentils, peas, and chickpeas are a tasty and versatile type of legume called *pulses*. Unlike other legume pods that are fresh-harvested or fatty (such as fresh beans, fresh peas, peanuts, and soybeans), pulses are harvested after they've dried on the plant, within their pods. The dehydrated seeds are an inexpensive protein source you can store for years, making them a pantry staple. Once rehydrated and cooked, they can be enjoyed in a host of applications, from sweet to savory. Whether they're braised, roasted, sprouted, or puréed, pulses are embraced by vegetarians, vegans, and omnivores alike for their nutrition, convenience, and flavor.

THEY'RE GOOD FOR YOU

High in essential vitamins and minerals but low in fat, dried legumes are widely considered to be a superfood that can help to prevent disease and contribute to a long, healthy life. They are particularly good sources of fiber and protein, a pairing that provides sustained energy but keeps cholesterol levels low. Beans, chickpeas, peas, and lentils contain between 20 and 25 percent protein by weight, much more than other popular plant-based protein sources, such as spinach and quinoa. This makes them an attractive alternative to meat-based proteins, particularly for vegans and vegetarians. Dried legumes are also rich in key minerals such as iron, potassium, zinc, and manganese, all of which play important roles in maintaining health.

HEALTH BENEFITS

Preserve heart health
Cholesterol-free and low in fat, pulses reduce the risk of heart disease.

Boost energy
Pulses are rich in iron, which helps transport oxygen in the bloodstream to rejuvenate your cells.

Build strong bones
Dense in manganese and other important nutrients, pulses promote healthy bone structure.

Maintain the gut
Pulses are fiber-packed and high in prebiotics, your body's natural digestive regulators.

Improve brain function
Because they're high in folic acid, pulses can improve mental and emotional health.

Aid weight loss
Pulses contain amino acids that boost metabolism as well as soluble fiber to make you feel fuller, longer.

Control blood sugar
Pulses are complex carbohydrates that provide steady glucose release to regulate insulin in the blood.

GREATER WATER EFFICIENCY

Legume crops are well-adapted to semi-arid climates and are more drought-tolerant than other crops. They require less water for cultivation than other plants and livestock. They also use water differently from other crops, drawing water from the shallow depth of the soil and leaving the deeper water in place for the next year's growth.

INCREASED FOOD SECURITY

For many people, regular access to meat, dairy, and fish may be cost prohibitive. Dried legumes provide a safe and nutritious food at a low cost, and their long shelf life means you can store them for months and even for years without losing nutritional value or expiring. Especially in developing countries, pulses can lift farmers out of rural poverty. Pulses can command prices two to three times higher than cereal crops, and their processing provides local job opportunities.

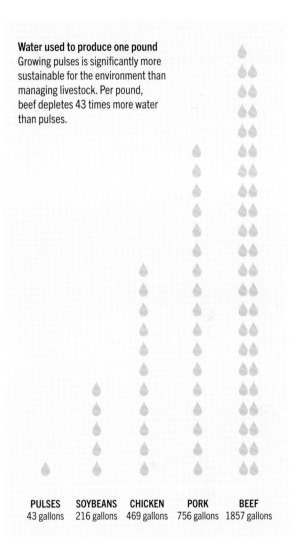

Water used to produce one pound
Growing pulses is significantly more sustainable for the environment than managing livestock. Per pound, beef depletes 43 times more water than pulses.

PULSES	SOYBEANS	CHICKEN	PORK	BEEF
43 gallons	216 gallons	469 gallons	756 gallons	1857 gallons

REDUCED CARBON FOOTPRINT

It takes energy to produce food, and that energy generates greenhouse gas emissions. However, legumes are more eco-friendly than other foods because they require no nitrogen fertilizer. Nitrogen fertilizer uses energy-intensive production processes and emits nitrous oxide, which has nearly 300 times the global warming potential of carbon dioxide.

HIGHER CROP YIELDS

Farmers all across the world know how important legumes are to their sustainable farming systems. Unlike most crops, pulses extract nitrogen from the air around them and fix it to the soil, leaving behind nitrogen-rich residues and other compounds that help fight disease and insects. This enriches the soil, making it possible for the next crop in rotation to produce higher yields.

BEANS

From the common to the exotic, there are many types of dried beans to cook and enjoy. Seek out unfamiliar varieties to experience the range of flavors and textures.

NAVY BEAN

Also called pea bean, white bean, white pea bean, and pearl haricot bean

Small and creamy, the navy bean is slightly flattened and oval shaped. It's excellent for baked beans, soups, dips, and spreads. In addition to lots of heart-healthy protein, the navy bean is full of dietary fiber that helps stabilize blood sugar.

BLACK-EYED PEA

Also called cow pea, California buckeye, and purple hull pea

Grown all over the world, the black-eyed pea shows off its single, prominent spot before being cooked. It appears in salads, rice dishes, and soups, and it complements bold flavors.

ADZUKI BEAN

Also called azuki bean and aduki bean

This small burgundy-colored bean originated in Asia. Its mild flavor lends the bean to sweet preparations; red bean paste is common in many Asian desserts. Also use it as you would the black bean in soups and chilis.

PINTO BEAN

Also called speckled bean and strawberry bean

Spanish for "painted," this medium-sized bean is speckled beige and red. When cooked, the specks disappear and the bean turns bright pink. It's perfect for refried beans and chili.

KIDNEY BEAN

Also called red bean

This medium-sized red bean resembles a kidney in shape and color. It is commonly found both dried and canned and is often used in soups and chilis. High in fiber and protein, kidney beans contribute to a healthy heart.

LIMA BEAN

Also called butter bean and sieva bean

Dried lima beans are flat, kidney-shaped, and white. The lima bean has a creamy texture, which lends it to inclusion in dips and traditional succotash recipes. Despite its rich texture, the lima bean is a nearly fat-free source of protein and fiber.

BLACK BEAN

Also called black turtle bean

Shiny and black, this bean earns its nickname "turtle" because of its smooth shell exterior. The black bean's meaty texture and mild taste makes it perfect for vegetarian recipes. It's commonly found in soups and served with rice in many cultures.

GREAT NORTHERN BEAN

Also called cannellini bean and white bean

This medium-sized flat bean has a creamy, off-white color. Its hearty texture makes it a natural addition to soups and stews, as well as braises and casseroles. It's an especially good substitute for the similar navy bean and an excellent source of protein and fiber.

MUNG BEAN

Also called moong bean and green gram

This small green bean is used in both sweet and savory applications. It is commonly found in Indian and Asian cooking. It's also easily sprouted, usually called "bean sprouts" in recipes.

MOTH BEAN

Also called moath bean, moat bean, matki, mat bean, and Turkish gram

Cultivated in many parts of the world, from India to Italy, the moth bean is a small, light brown cylindrical pulse with a nutty flavor. Its flavor profile complements aromatic spices, coconut, and foods with a touch of sweetness.

SCARLET RUNNER

Also called runner bean and multiflora bean

Originally from Mexico, the scarlet runner bean is one of the oldest cultivated foods of the Americas. The large bean is a striking purple and black color and has a dense, meaty texture. It's best used in stews, casseroles, and chilis.

BLACK GRAM

Also called vinga mungo, black lentil, black urad dal, and mungo bean

Most often used in Indian cooking, the black gram is a small black cylindrical bean with a creamy white interior. The deep, earthy flavor makes it a perfect match for curries, stews, and other boldly flavored dishes.

HEIRLOOM BEANS

Untouched by genetic science, there are endless varieties of heirloom beans, each with a unique look and depth of flavor. They are cultivated in a single setting for generations, never mass-produced, so the genetic pureness produces the same seed with each generation of planting. Heirlooms are not usually on the shelves of ordinary stores, but when you do find them, they are a culinary delight.

LENTILS, CHICKPEAS, PEAS & FLOURS

It's not just beans that revolutionize your cooking! Lentils and peas are great because they don't require pre-soaking. You can also grind some pulses into flours, a perfect swap for gluten-sensitive individuals.

BROWN LENTIL

Varieties include Spanish pardina, German brown, Indian brown, and brewer lentil

The most common type of lentil, it ranges from a light khaki color to a deep, ruddy brown. This lentil has a creamy, slightly nutty taste that works in a variety of cuisines. Moderately firm, it can either hold its shape in soups and casseroles or mash easily for burgers and patties.

YELLOW LENTIL

Also called golden lentil, toor dal, arhar dal, and tan lentils

Similar to red lentils, the yellow lentil is mild, sweet, and faintly nutty. It disintegrates quickly during cooking, which works well in spreads and soups. You'll often find yellow lentils in Indian dishes such as curries and dal.

RED LENTIL

Also called petite red lentil, crimson lentil, and red chief

Mild and slightly sweet, this lentil is pinkish-orange and sold both whole and split. Since it's very small, it breaks down quickly once cooked and is ideal for soups and dips. You can even use red lentils as a thickening agent for gravies and stews.

GREEN LENTIL

Also called Le Puy lentil, Lentilles du Puy, and French green lentil

The green lentil has a rich, deep flavor and holds its shape well after cooking. Use it in salads, stews, and casseroles to accentuate its firm texture.

BELUGA LENTIL

Also called black lentil and petite beluga lentil

The shiny and small black lentil is named after the caviar it resembles. The beluga lentil is mild in flavor and holds its shape when cooked, making it a great ingredient for salads, pilafs, and stuffings.

CHICKPEA

Also called garbanzo bean, gram, Bengal gram, chana dal, and kabuli

There are two types of chickpeas—desi and kabuli—but the more common kabuli is the large, pale variety usually just labeled "chickpea." The chickpea (not actually a true pea) has a soft, creamy texture perfect for spreads.

PIGEON PEA

Also called split toor dal

The pigeon pea is nutty and crisp. It's a key food source around the world—hearty, drought resistant, and cultivated for over 3,000 years. The small, glossy brown pea is often served alongside rice.

SPLIT PEA

Varieties include green split pea and yellow split pea

The split pea is harvested whole then split in half. It is similar in taste and texture to lentils but rounder in shape and brighter in color. It's best known for making soups and Indian dal, but also works well in dips and spreads.

CHICKPEA FLOUR

This is one of the most versatile legume flours. It's creamy, sweet, and slightly nutty, making chickpea flour a great addition to baked goods and pizza crust. Use it in recipes that contain bold flavors like pumpkin bread or Middle Eastern fare.

WHITE BEAN FLOUR

This flour is extremely mild. When combined with stabilizers such as xanthan gum or potato starch, white bean flour is an excellent substitute in gluten-free baking. The creamy mild texture makes it a natural addition to soups, sauces, and gravies.

HOW TO COOK

You can cook pulses on the stove or in a slow cooker or pressure cooker. For optimal flavor, use stock instead of water and add bay leaves, onions, garlic, and other aromatics. Just don't add salt until the last 30 minutes or you'll prolong the cooking time.

1. PREPARE Sort the pulses on a tray, removing broken and irregular pieces or small stones. Then remove dirt and grit by rinsing the pulses under water in a fine mesh sieve.

2. PRESOAK Place the pulses in a large bowl and cover with cool water about 2 inches (5cm) above the level of the pulses. Most should soak for 8 hours or overnight.

3. DRAIN & RINSE Drain and rinse again in a fine mesh sieve under cool water to wash away impurities or toxins released by soaking.

4. COOK Transfer the pulses to a stockpot. Cover with water or stock at least 2 inches (5cm) above the level of the pulses. Bring to a boil and then reduce to a simmer. Cook per the pulse's cooking time (see right). Skim off any foam that develops on the surface.

5. CHECK For a perfectly cooked batch, check on your pulses within the suggested cooking time range by pinching and tasting a few. A perfectly cooked pulse yields easily when pinched and is soft throughout while maintaining shape. An undercooked pulse will not give when pinched. An overcooked pulse loses its shape, but you can still salvage the batch for dips, spreads, and purées.

		PRESOAK TIME	STOVETOP SIMMER TIME
PEAS	**Chickpea**	8 hrs–overnight	1 hr–90 mins
	Pigeon pea	8 hrs–overnight	45 mins–1 hr
	Split pea	Not required	30 mins
LENTILS	**Beluga lentil**	Not required	25 mins
	Brown lentil	Not required	20–25 mins
	Green lentil	Not required	20–25 mins
	Red lentil	Not required	15–20 mins
	Yellow lentil	Not required	15–20 mins
BEANS	**Adzuki bean**	1–2 hrs	45 mins–1 hr
	Black bean	8 hrs–overnight	45 mins–1 hr
	Black-eyed pea	8 hrs–overnight	1 hr
	Black gram	8 hrs–overnight	30 mins
	Great northern bean	8 hrs–overnight	1 hr
	Kidney bean	8 hrs–overnight	1 hr–90 mins
	Lima bean	8 hrs–overnight	1 hr
	Moth bean	8 hrs–overnight	20–25 mins
	Mung bean	Not required	30–45 mins
	Navy bean	8 hrs–overnight	1 hr–90 mins
	Pinto bean	8 hrs–overnight	1 hr–75 mins
	Scarlet runner	8 hrs–overnight	90 mins

NOTE: Bolded pulses are suitable for sprouting.

PRESSURE COOKER TIME (ON HIGH)	SLOW COOKER TIME (ON LOW)	GOOD SUBSTITUTES
10–12 mins	6–8 hrs	Great northern bean
6–9 mins	2–3 hrs	Black-eyed pea
1 min	6–8 hrs	Green lentil
1 min	6–7 hrs	Brown lentil, green lentil
1 min	6–7 hrs	Beluga lentil, green lentil
1 min	6–7 hrs	Beluga lentil, brown lentil
1 min	6–7 hrs	Yellow lentil
1 min	6–7 hrs	Red lentil
5–9 mins	6–8 hrs	Mung bean
9–11 mins	6–8 hrs	Borlotti bean, pinto bean, navy bean
3–5 mins	6–8 hrs	Pigeon pea
7 mins	6–8 hrs	Moth bean
8–12 mins	6–8 hrs	Navy bean
6–8 mins	6–7 hrs	Great Northern bean
4–7 mins	6–7 hrs	Navy bean
5–6 mins	4–6 hrs	Black gram, beluga lentil
5–9 mins	6–8 hrs	Adzuki bean
6–8 mins	6–7 hrs	Great northern bean
4–6 mins	6–7 hrs	Kidney bean, borlotti bean
5–8 mins	5–7 hrs	Kidney bean

HOW TO SPROUT

Sprouted pulses are fresh, crisp, and bursting with nutrients. Before getting started, be sure to select a pulse variety that is suitable for sprouting; they are shown in bold type in the table on the left.

1. In a large jar, generously cover the pulses with filtered water. Cover the mouth of the jar with cheese cloth and secure with a rubber band or twine. Soak in a cool, dark place for 8 hours or overnight.

2. Drain the jar. Run fresh water through to rinse the pulses once or twice. Cover the mouth of the jar again. Tip the jar sideways and let the water fully drain.

3. Return to the storage space on its side, covered with cheese cloth, with the base elevated to allow the pulses to sprout. About every 12 hours, repeat step 2 and return to the storage space.

4. When the sprouts reach the desired length, remove from the jar and dry. Most varieties require 2 to 4 days to reach an average length. Store in an airtight bag in the refrigerator.

USING CANNED BEANS Use canned beans in place of home-cooked beans in any recipe. A 15-ounce (425g) can contains about 1½ cups of prepared beans. Be sure to thoroughly rinse them before using because the packaging liquid can nearly double the sodium content.

BREAKFAST

CURRIED MUNG BEAN AVOCADO TOAST

Sprouts and mung beans elevate your breakfast toast to the next level of tasty. The hint of curry flavor works well with the creamy, smooth avocado.

MAKES 3 ▪ PREP 10 MINS ▪ COOK 4 MINS

3 slices sourdough or whole wheat country bread

1 avocado, divided

1 cup cooked mung beans

½ tsp curry powder

Pinch turmeric

Salt and pepper

¾ cup sprouted mung beans

3 tbsp chopped chives

1. Toast the bread until browned and crispy.

2. Cut the avocado in half and remove the pit. Scoop out the flesh of one half and add to a medium mixing bowl. With a potato masher, mash avocado half.

3. Stir in the mung beans, curry powder, and turmeric. Taste and season with salt and pepper. Spread the avocado mixture evenly over the slices of toast.

4. Remove the flesh from the remaining avocado half and thinly slice. Arrange equal amounts atop each slice of toast.

5. Place on serving plates and top with equal amounts of sprouted mung beans and chives. Serve immediately.

MAKE IT WITH MEAT Crumble 2 slices cooked bacon into the avocado–mung bean mixture.

Nutrition per toast
Calories 330 | Total Fat 9g | Saturated Fat 1.5g | Cholesterol 0mg | Sodium 340mg | Total Carbohydrate 53g | Dietary Fiber 9g | Sugars 4g | Protein 14g

LENTIL CREAM CHEESE TARTINES

Flavored cream cheese is so easy to make at home. Adding lentils, chives, and lemon zest to the rich spread creates great texture for the simple breakfast dish.

MAKES 6 ▪ PREP 10 MINS ▪ COOK 20 MINS

6 slices whole wheat bread

8oz (225g) cream cheese, softened

¾ cup cooked brown lentils

2 tbsp chopped chives

Zest of 1 lemon

Salt and pepper

3 tsp olive oil, divided

6 large eggs

2 cups watercress

1. Preheat the oven to 300°F (150°C). Arrange the slices of bread on a baking sheet. Toast for 5 minutes, flip, and toast for another 5 minutes or until crispy and golden.

2. Meanwhile, make the cream cheese spread. In a food processor, blend the cream cheese, lentils, chives, and lemon zest until thoroughly combined. Season with salt and pepper to taste. Spread the cream cheese mixture evenly over the slices of toast.

3. In a nonstick skillet, heat 1 teaspoon oil over medium-low heat until hot. Crack 2 eggs into the skillet and cook for 5 minutes or until the whites are set but the yolks are runny. Place each cooked egg atop a slice of toast. Repeat with the remaining olive oil and eggs. Top each tartine with ⅓ cup watercress and serve immediately.

MAKE IT WITH MEAT Top each tartine with 1 ounce (28g) smoked salmon, thinly sliced.

Nutrition per tartine
Calories 280 | Total Fat 17g | Saturated Fat 8g | Cholesterol 40mg | Sodium 400mg | Total Carbohydrates 22g | Dietary Fiber 4g | Sugars 4g | Protein 13g

ROASTED TOMATO & CHICKPEA FRITTATA

Frittatas are a wonderful way to feed a crowd for breakfast or brunch. Chickpeas add an unexpected twist and extra body to this morning classic.

SERVES 10 ▪ PREP 15 MINS ▪ COOK 30 MINS

2 cups (about 475g) grape tomatoes

1 garlic clove, minced

2 thyme sprigs

1 tbsp olive oil

10 large eggs

2 tbsp heavy cream

2 tsp chopped chives

Salt and pepper

3 cups baby spinach

2 cups cooked chickpeas

1. Preheat the oven to 400°F (200°C). On a rimmed baking sheet, toss the tomatoes, garlic, and thyme in the oil. Spread in an even layer and roast for 10 minutes. Discard the thyme sprigs. Let cool slightly.

2. Meanwhile, in a large mixing bowl, whisk together the eggs, heavy cream, and chives. Season with salt and pepper to taste.

3. Heat a 10-inch (25cm) cast-iron or ovenproof skillet over medium heat. Transfer the roasted tomato mixture to the skillet. Add the spinach and cook for 1 to 2 minutes or until the spinach slightly wilts. Add the chickpeas and stir to combine. Spread the mixture evenly in the skillet.

4. Pour the egg mixture over the tomatoes, spinach, and chickpeas. Cook over medium heat, uncovered, for 2 to 3 minutes or until the edges of the egg begin to set. Transfer the skillet to the oven and cook, uncovered, for an additional 8 to 10 minutes or until the edges are set but the center is still slightly springy. Slice into 10 wedges and serve immediately.

MAKE IT WITH MEAT Add 5 ounces (140g) finely diced ham or chicken sausage, cooked, to the skillet with chickpeas in step 3.

WHY NOT TRY... For a creamy tang, sprinkle 4 ounces (110g) goat cheese over the egg mixture before baking.

Nutrition per serving
Calories 130 | Total Fat 8g | Saturated Fat 2.5g | Cholesterol 190mg | Sodium 360mg |
Total Carbohydrate 7g | Dietary Fiber 2g | Sugars 2g | Protein 8g

BLACK-EYED PEA CHILAQUILES

This traditional Mexican dish is an excellent way to use leftover tortillas. Baked with black-eyed peas and a savory, spicy tomato sauce, tortillas are transformed into breakfast comfort food.

SERVES 4 ▪ PREP 20 MINS ▪ COOK 45 MINS

8 small white corn tortillas, each cut into six wedges

3 tbsp vegetable oil

2 garlic cloves, minced

1½ tsp dried oregano

3 tsp ancho chili powder

1½ tsp ground cumin

½ tsp cayenne

1 (15oz/227g) can tomato sauce

1 cup water

1 cup cooked black-eyed peas

6oz (170g) crumbled queso fresco or Cotija cheese

3 green onions, chopped

1 small jalapeño, thinly sliced

1 cup cilantro leaves

1. Preheat the oven to 325°F (170°C). To make tortilla chips, toss the cut tortilla pieces in 2 tablespoons oil. Arrange on a baking sheet and bake for 15 to 20 minutes or until crispy and golden brown.

2. Meanwhile, make the sauce. In a medium saucepan, heat the remaining 1 tablespoon oil over medium-low heat. Add the garlic and cook for 1 to 2 minutes or until soft but not browned. Stir in the oregano, ancho chili powder, cumin, cayenne, tomato sauce, and water. Bring to a boil and then reduce the heat and simmer for 15 minutes or until the sauce is slightly thickened.

3. In a large mixing bowl, toss the tortilla chips with the black-eyed peas and about two-thirds of the sauce. Arrange in an even layer in a baking dish. Sprinkle the queso fresco on top. Bake for 8 to 10 minutes or until the cheese is melted.

4. Garnish with the green onion, jalapeño, and cilantro. Serve immediately with the remaining sauce on the side.

MAKE IT WITH MEAT Layer in 4½ ounces (130g) cooked, shredded chicken or pork before adding the cheese in step 3.

WHY NOT TRY... Top with one runny, over-easy egg per portion.

Nutrition per serving
Calories 380 | Total Fat 18g | Saturated Fat 11g | Cholesterol 45mg | Sodium 750mg | Total Carbohydrate 41g | Dietary Fiber 7g | Sugars 6g | Protein 15g

ENGLISH BREAKFAST EGG-IN-THE-HOLE

This mash-up of the traditional English breakfast and egg-in-the-hole is an unexpected way to unite the two breakfast classics.

SERVES 4 ▪ PREP 20 MINS ▪ COOK 40 MINS

1 tbsp olive oil

1 small yellow onion, finely diced

1 garlic clove, minced

2 cups cooked navy beans

1¼ cups tomato purée

2 tbsp molasses

Pinch of red pepper flakes

Salt and pepper

2 Roma tomatoes, halved lengthwise

2 cups quartered white mushrooms

4 slices whole wheat bread

4 large eggs

1. Prepare the baked beans. In a medium saucepan, heat the oil over medium heat. Add the onion and cook for 5 minutes. Add the garlic and cook for an additional minute.

2. Stir in the navy beans, tomato purée, molasses, and red pepper flakes. Bring to a boil and then reduce to a simmer and cook for 20 minutes. Taste and season with salt and pepper.

3. Meanwhile, heat a large nonstick skillet over medium heat. Sear the tomatoes, cut-side down, for 3 to 4 minutes or until lightly cooked. Remove and set aside on serving plates. Then add the mushrooms to the skillet. Season with salt and pepper and cook for 3 to 4 minutes or until tender. Remove and place on the serving plates. Wipe out the skillet and return to the stove over medium-low heat.

4. Cut a 2-inch (5cm) round hole from the center of each slice of bread. Place two slices of bread, along with the cut-out circles, in the skillet. Cook until toasted on one side, and then flip over. Crack one egg into each hole and cook for 3 to 5 minutes or until the whites are set and the yolks are cooked to the desired doneness. Remove to the serving plates and repeat with the remaining bread and eggs.

5. Top each egg-in-the-hole with baked beans and serve immediately with the cut-out center for dipping.

Nutrition per serving
Calories 380 | Total Fat 10g | Saturated Fat 2.5g | Cholesterol 185mg | Sodium 230mg |
Total Carbohydrate 54g | Dietary Fiber 14g | Sugars 15g | Protein 20g

BLACK BEAN BREAKFAST TOSTADAS

These crunchy fried tortillas are topped with creamy scrambled eggs and spicy seasoned black beans for an irresistible savory breakfast.

SERVES 4 ▪ PREP 15 MINS ▪ COOK 25 MINS

1 tbsp olive oil

1 small white onion, finely diced

1 jalapeño, deseeded and finely diced

1 garlic clove, minced

2 cups cooked black beans

1 tbsp ground cumin

1 tsp chipotle chili powder

½ cup vegetable stock

Salt and pepper

4 corn tostada shells

4 large eggs

½ tbsp heavy cream

4oz (110g) Cotija cheese

Cilantro, to garnish

Hot sauce, to serve

1. Preheat the oven to 325°F (170°C). In a medium skillet, heat the oil over medium heat until shimmering. Add the onion and cook for 5 to 10 minutes or until softened. Add the jalapeño and garlic and cook for an additional 2 to 3 minutes.

2. Add the black beans, cumin, and chipotle chili powder and stir to coat. Add the stock, bring to boil, and then reduce to a simmer and cook for 5 minutes or until the liquid reduces. Taste and season with salt and pepper.

3. Meanwhile, on a rimmed baking sheet, arrange the tostada shells in an even layer with edges slightly overlapping. Bake for 2 to 3 minutes or until warmed through.

4. In a small mixing bowl, whisk together the eggs and heavy cream. In a nonstick skillet over medium-low heat, scramble the eggs to the desired consistency.

5. To assemble, spread equal amounts of the black bean mixture on the tostada shells. Top with equal amounts scrambled eggs. Sprinkle 1 ounce (25g) Cotija cheese on each tostada. Garnish with fresh cilantro and serve immediately with hot sauce.

MAKE IT VEGAN Instead of eggs, scramble 8 ounces (225g) firm tofu with salt and pepper.

WHY NOT TRY... For a boost of healthy fats, top each tostada with wedges of sliced avocado.

Nutrition per serving
Calories 430 | Total Fat 22g | Saturated Fat 8g | Cholesterol 220mg | Sodium 500mg |
Total Carbohydrate 37g | Dietary Fiber 9g | Sugars 3g | Protein 21g

RED LENTIL SHAKSHUKA

This comforting Mediterranean one-skillet meal is an easy-to-make breakfast of eggs baked in spicy tomato sauce. The red lentils add a hearty texture and nutty taste.

SERVES 4 ▪ PREP 25 MINS ▪ COOK 35 MINS

2 tbsp olive oil

1 small yellow onion, diced

1 red bell pepper, deseeded and chopped

2 garlic cloves, minced

1 Thai chile, deseeded and minced

1 (14oz/400g) can petite diced tomatoes (undrained)

1 (14oz/400g) can crushed tomatoes

1 tbsp tomato paste

1 tsp ground cumin

¾ tsp smoked paprika

2 tbsp red wine vinegar

¼ cup dried red lentils

Salt and pepper

4 large eggs

3 tbsp chopped flat-leaf parsley

1. In a 10-inch (25cm) cast-iron skillet, warm the oil over medium heat until shimmering. Add the onion and bell pepper and cook for 5 to 10 minutes or until softened. Add the garlic and chile and continue to cook for 1 to 2 minutes or until fragrant.

2. Add the diced tomatoes, crushed tomatoes, tomato paste, cumin, paprika, and vinegar, and stir to combine. Cook for 5 minutes or until warmed through. Add the lentils and cook, covered, for 20 to 25 minutes or until the lentils are tender. Season with salt and pepper to taste.

3. With the back of a spoon, create 4 wells in the tomato-lentil mixture. Crack one egg into each well. Cover the skillet and cook for 5 to 8 minutes or until the eggs are just set. Sprinkle with parsley and serve immediately.

MAKE IT VEGAN Omit the eggs and use tofu rounds, firmly pressed and cut into 4½-inch (11cm) slices.

Nutrition per serving
Calories 240 | Total Fat 12g | Saturated Fat 2.5g | Cholesterol 185mg | Sodium 280mg | Total Carbohydrate 21g | Dietary Fiber 5g | Sugars 8g | Protein 11g

ASPARAGUS & GREEN LENTILS
WITH POACHED EGG

This impressive-looking brunch dish couldn't be easier to prepare. The yolk from the poached egg makes a luxurious sauce over the roasted asparagus and lentils.

SERVES 4 ▪ PREP 10 MINS ▪ COOK 15 MINS

1lb (450g) thin asparagus, woody ends removed

2 tbsp olive oil, divided

Salt and pepper

2½ tbsp red wine vinegar

1 tbsp Dijon mustard

¼ tsp chopped thyme

1⅓ cups cooked green lentils

Dash of white vinegar

4 large eggs

1. Preheat the oven to 350°F (180°C). Toss the asparagus with 1 tablespoon oil. Arrange on a baking sheet in a single layer and season with salt and pepper. Roast for 10 minutes or until tender.

2. Meanwhile, make the dressing. In a medium bowl, combine the red wine vinegar, Dijon mustard, thyme, and remaining 1 tablespoon oil. Whisk until emulsified. Add the lentils and stir to combine. Set aside and let the lentils absorb the dressing.

3. To poach the eggs, fill a large saucepan with water about 1½-inches (4cm) deep. Bring the water to a boil then reduce to a very gentle simmer. Add the white vinegar. One at a time, crack an egg into a ramekin and gently tip the egg into the water. Cook for 3 minutes. Remove and place on a plate lined with paper towel to absorb water.

4. To serve, arrange the asparagus among the serving plates and top each with dressed lentils. Place one poached egg atop each plate. Season with pepper and serve immediately.

Nutrition per serving
Calories 238 | Total Fat 12.5g | Saturated Fat 2.6g | Cholesterol 183mg | Sodium 195mg | Total Carbohydrate 19g | Dietary Fiber 6g | Sugars 3.7g | Protein 15g

CHICKPEA & ROOT VEGETABLE HASH

This breakfast hash elevates simple root vegetables and makes them the star. A luscious egg yolk creates a rich sauce for the roasted vegetables.

SERVES 6 ▪ PREP 20 MINS ▪ COOK 30 MINS

2 tbsp coconut oil

1 small sweet potato, peeled and diced

1 medium turnip, peeled and diced

1 large parsnip, peeled and diced

3 carrots, diced

1 tbsp thyme

Pinch of red pepper flakes

½ tsp ancho chili powder

2 cups cooked chickpeas

Salt and pepper

6 large eggs

1. Preheat the oven to 375°F (190°C). In a large cast-iron skillet, heat the oil over medium heat. Once shimmering, add the sweet potato, turnip, parsnip, and carrots. Stir to coat.

2. Add the thyme, red pepper flakes, and ancho chili powder. Stir once more, and then place the skillet in the oven and cook for 20 minutes or until the vegetables are tender. Remove from the oven, add the chickpeas, stir, and return to the oven. Cook for an additional 5 minutes or until the chickpeas are warmed through.

3. Meanwhile, heat a large nonstick skillet over medium heat. Working in batches as needed, crack the eggs into the skillet and cook for 3 minutes, or until the whites are set but the yolks are runny.

4. Taste and season the hash with salt and pepper. Divide between 6 serving plates and top each with an egg. Serve immediately.

MAKE IT WITH MEAT Sauté ⅓ cup diced pancetta in coconut oil until slightly crispy. Add along with the root vegetables in step 1.

Nutrition per serving
Calories 260 | Total Fat 11g | Saturated Fat 6g | Cholesterol 185mg | Sodium 320mg |
Total Carbohydrate 28g | Dietary Fiber 7g | Sugars 7g | Protein 12g |

LEMON POPPY SEED PANCAKES

Poppy seeds add unexpected texture to these fluffy, flavorful pancakes.

MAKES 4 ▪ PREP 30 MINS ▪ COOK 20 MINS

¾ cup unsweetened almond milk

3 tbsp lemon juice

Zest of 2 lemons

2 tbsp melted and cooled coconut oil

1 tsp vanilla extract

2½ tbsp granulated sugar

1 tsp baking soda

1 tsp baking powder

1 cup chickpea flour

1 tbsp poppy seeds

1. In a small mixing bowl, stir together the almond milk, lemon juice, lemon zest, coconut oil, vanilla, and sugar.

2. In a large mixing bowl, whisk together the baking soda, baking powder, and chickpea flour. Pour the almond milk mixture into flour mixture and gently stir just until smooth. Gently fold in the poppy seeds. Let the batter rest for 10 minutes without stirring.

3. Heat a medium nonstick skillet or griddle over medium heat. Pour about a quarter of the batter into the skillet. Cook for 2 minutes or until bubbles form along the outer edge and throughout the middle. Gently flip and cook for an additional 1 to 2 minutes. Remove from the heat and repeat with remaining batter to make 4 pancakes total. Serve immediately with butter or maple syrup.

Nutrition per pancake
Calories 140 | Total Fat 7g | Saturated Fat 4g | Cholesterol 0mg | Sodium 240mg |
Total Carbohydrate 16g | Dietary Fiber 2g | Sugars 6g | Protein 4g

CINNAMON RAISIN BREAKFAST QUINOA

Quinoa and lentils can be breakfast food, too! With the warm flavors of vanilla, cinnamon, and almond, this dish is as comforting as oatmeal but with more protein.

SERVES 6 ▪ PREP 10 MINS ▪ COOK 35 MINS

1 cup dried quinoa

1 large vanilla bean

4 cups unsweetened almond milk, plus extra to serve

¼ cup agave nectar or honey

1 cinnamon stick

¼ tsp ground nutmeg

½ cup dried yellow lentils

1 cup raisins

1 cup chopped almonds

Fresh berries (optional), to serve

1. Thoroughly rinse the quinoa in a fine mesh strainer. Let air dry slightly.

2. Cut the vanilla bean lengthwise down the middle. Scrape out the vanilla seeds. Reserve both the seeds and pod.

3. In a medium saucepan, combine the almond milk, agave, cinnamon stick, nutmeg, vanilla seeds, and vanilla pod. Bring to a gentle boil. Add the quinoa and lentils. Cook, covered, for 20 to 25 minutes or until the lentils and quinoa are tender and most of the liquid is absorbed. Remove the vanilla pod and cinnamon stick.

4. To serve, portion into six bowls. Drizzle with additional almond milk (if desired), and top each bowl with equal amounts raisins, chopped almonds, and fresh berries.

Nutrition per serving
Calories 410 | Total Fat 13g | Saturated Fat 1g | Cholesterol 0mg | Sodium 110mg | Total Carbohydrate 65g | Dietary Fiber 7g | Sugars 29g | Protein 13g

SPICED APPLE & MUNG BEAN MUFFINS

Mung beans puréed with applesauce make for one of the moistest muffins you'll ever taste. The protein- and fiber-filled breakfast is perfect when you're on-the-go.

MAKES 12 ▪ PREP 35 MINS ▪ COOK 20 MINS

⅔ cup unsweetened applesauce

½ cup cooked mung beans

2 tbsp agave nectar

¾ cup whole wheat flour

¾ cup all-purpose flour

2 tsp baking powder

1 tsp cinnamon

Pinch of ground nutmeg

1 large egg

½ cup firmly packed light brown sugar

⅓ cup unsweetened almond milk

1 medium Granny Smith apple, peeled, cored, and finely diced (about 1 cup)

¼ cup old-fashioned rolled oats

1. Preheat the oven to 350°F (175°C). In a food processor, purée the applesauce, mung beans, and agave until smooth.

2. In a large mixing bowl, whisk together the whole wheat flour, all-purpose flour, baking powder, cinnamon, and nutmeg.

3. In a medium mixing bowl, add the egg, brown sugar, almond milk, and applesauce–mung bean mixture. Whisk to combine.

4. Add the egg–mung bean mixture to the flour mixture and stir just until no streaks of dry ingredients remain. Gently fold in the diced apples.

5. Line a 12-cup muffin pan with paper liners. Portion 2 tablespoons batter into each cup. Sprinkle the top of each muffin with 1 teaspoon oats. Bake for 20 to 25 minutes or until set and a toothpick inserted into the center of a muffin comes out clean. Let cool for an hour before serving. Store in an airtight container on the counter for up to 2 days.

MAKE IT VEGAN Substitute ¼ cup mashed banana instead of the egg.

Nutrition per muffin
Calories 110 | Total Fat 0.5g | Saturated Fat 0g | Cholesterol 0mg | Sodium 5mg | Total Carbohydrate 25g | Dietary Fiber 2g | Sugars 10g | Protein 2g

YELLOW LENTIL WAFFLES
WITH FIVE SPICE BERRY SAUCE

Crispy on the outside and soft on the inside, these mild waffles will fill all your breakfast cravings. The five spice in the sauce makes the sweetness of the berries sing.

MAKES 4 ▪ PREP 15 MINS ▪ COOK 15 MINS

6oz (170g) fresh raspberries, plus more to serve

6oz (170g) fresh blackberries, plus more to serve

6oz (170g) fresh blueberries, plus more to serve

¼ tsp five spice powder

1 cinnamon stick

3 tbsp water (as needed)

1¼ cups unsweetened almond milk

¼ cup canola oil

2 tsp vanilla extract

3 tbsp agave nectar

1½ cups whole wheat flour

1½ tsp baking powder

½ cup cooked yellow lentils

1. In a small saucepan, combine the raspberries, blackberries, blueberries, five spice powder, and cinnamon stick. Cook, covered and stirring regularly, over low heat for 15 minutes or until the berries break down into a thickened sauce. Add 2 to 3 tablespoons water as needed.

2. Meanwhile, in a small bowl, whisk together the almond milk, oil, vanilla, and agave.

3. Preheat a waffle maker. In a large mixing bowl, combine the whole wheat flour and baking powder. Stir in the almond milk mixture. Gently fold in the lentils.

4. Once heated, spray each section of the waffle iron with cooking spray. Portion the batter into the waffle maker and cook according to the manufacturer's instructions. The batter makes 4 (½ cup) waffles total.

5. Remove the cinnamon stick from the sauce. Serve the waffles immediately with the sauce and fresh berries.

Nutrition per waffle
Calories 350 | Total Fat 10g | Saturated Fat 0.5g | Cholesterol 0mg | Sodium 80mg |
Total Carbohydrate 50g | Dietary Fiber 13g | Sugars 6g | Protein 13g

TROPICAL SMOOTHIE BOWL

The bright flavors of pineapple and mango are complemented by velvety white beans and banana in these beautiful protein-rich bowls.

SERVES 2 ▪ PREP 10 MINS

1 cup diced mango

1 cup diced pineapple

1 banana, sliced

1 tbsp honey or agave nectar

¾ cup low-fat vanilla yogurt

½ cup cooked great northern beans

¼ cup toasted coconut, to garnish

2 tsp chia seeds, to garnish

1. Withhold a bit of mango, pineapple, and banana for garnish. In a blender, add the remainder of the fruit along with the honey, yogurt, and great northern beans. Purée until completely smooth.

2. Portion the smoothie into two bowls and garnish with toasted coconut, chia seeds, and the reserved mango, pineapple, and banana. Serve immediately.

MAKE IT VEGAN Use a vegan yogurt alternative rather than vanilla yogurt.

Nutrition per serving
Calories 370 | Total Fat 7g | Saturated Fat 4.5g | Cholesterol <5mg | Sodium 95mg |
Total Carbohydrate 72g | Dietary Fiber 9g | Sugars 51g | Protein 9g

SNACKS & SPREADS

YELLOW LENTIL DEVILED EGGS

Basil, oregano, and lemon juice brighten these deviled eggs. Incorporating yellow lentils into the filling adds great texture for a modern take on the classic.

MAKES 12 • PREP 20 MINS • COOK 10 MINS

6 large eggs

⅓ cup cooked yellow lentils

¼ cup mayonnaise or sour cream

¾ tsp Dijon mustard

¼ cup chopped basil

¼ cup chopped oregano

½ tbsp lemon juice

Salt and pepper

Chopped chervil or chives, to garnish

1. Bring a large pot of water to a rolling boil and carefully lower the eggs into the water. Boil for 9 minutes, and then immediately remove the eggs to an ice bath to cool. Once completely cooled, peel off the shells and slice the eggs in half lengthwise.

2. To make the filling, in a food processor add the yolks, lentils, mayonnaise, mustard, basil, and oregano. Process on low speed while slowly drizzling in the lemon juice. Purée until smooth. Taste and season with salt and pepper.

3. Carefully spoon or pipe about 1 tablespoon of the filling into each egg half. Garnish with chervil or chives. Serve immediately or store in an airtight container in the refrigerator for up to 2 days.

MAKE IT WITH MEAT Garnish the deviled eggs with 2 tablespoons orange tobiko or another colorful caviar.

Nutrition per deviled egg

Calories 80 | Total Fat 6g | Saturated Fat 1.5g | Cholesterol 95mg | Sodium 160mg | Total Carbohydrate 3g | Dietary Fiber 1g | Sugars 0g | Protein 4g

SPIRALIZED BEET & ONION BHAJIS
WITH CUCUMBER SAUCE

These crispy Indian fritters are a delicious appetizer or snack. The spiralized beets in this version add a vivid maroon color.

MAKES 12 ▪ PREP 15 MINS ▪ COOK 15 MINS

1 quart canola oil

1 cup plain Greek yogurt

1 small cucumber, peeled and grated

1 large yellow onion, peeled

1 large beet, peeled

Dash of turmeric

½ tsp salt

¾ cup chickpea flour

½ cup water

1. In a large Dutch oven or heavy-bottomed pot, heat the canola oil over medium heat. Using a deep frying thermometer, bring the oil to 350°F (180°C).

2. While the oil heats, make the cucumber sauce. In a small bowl stir together the Greek yogurt and cucumber.

3. With a spiralizer or mandoline, slice the onion and beet into thin strips. With kitchen shears, trim the pieces into 1-inch (3cm) lengths.

4. In a large mixing bowl, whisk together the turmeric, salt, chickpea flour, and water. Gradually add water a few teaspoons at a time until the batter is the consistency of pancake batter. Add the beet and onion and toss to combine.

5. With your hands, gather 2 tablespoons bhaji mixture into a loose ball and carefully drop into the oil. Fry for 4 minutes or until golden and crispy, rotating once. Place on a plate lined with paper towel and repeat with the remaining batter. Serve immediately with the cucumber sauce.

MAKE IT VEGAN Substitute coconut milk yogurt.

Nutrition per bhaji
Calories 210 | Total Fat 19g | Saturated Fat 1.5g | Cholesterol 0mg | Sodium 110mg |
Total Carbohydrate 7g | Dietary Fiber 1g | Sugars 3g | Protein 4g |

ADZUKI BEAN SUMMER ROLLS
WITH PEANUT SAUCE

Spiralized jicama replaces traditional rice noodles in these summer rolls. Adzuki beans work well with the sweetness of the mango and the creaminess of the avocado.

MAKES 16 ▪ PREP 1 HR

½ cup creamy peanut butter

Juice of 1 lime

1 tbsp rice wine vinegar

⅓ cup water

½ tsp sriracha sauce

1 small jicama, peeled

1oz (25g) mint leaves

1 mango, peeled, pitted, and cut into ½-in (1cm) slices

1 small red onion, julienned

1 avocado, cut into ¼-in (½cm) slices

1½ cups cooked adzuki beans

2 cups cilantro leaves

1 (12oz/340g) pkg spring roll rice paper wrappers

1. Make the peanut sauce. In a small bowl, whisk together the peanut butter, lime juice, vinegar, water, and sriracha until smooth. Set aside until ready to serve.

2. Cut the jicama into even chunks. With a spiralizer or mandoline, slice the jicama into thin strips. Prepare your workspace with the jicama, mint, mango, onion, avocado, adzuki beans, and cilantro to assemble the rolls. You will also need a clean, flat surface on which the wrappers will not stick (such as a plastic or ceramic board).

3. Pour warm water into a shallow pie pan. Working one at a time, submerge the rice paper wrapper into the warm water for about 30 seconds or until pliable but will not tear. Place the wrapper onto the nonstick surface.

4. Arrange the desired amount mint leaves, mango, red onion, avocado, adzuki beans, cilantro, and jicama in the center of wrapper, being sure to work quickly so the wrapper doesn't dry. (Do not overstuff the ingredients or the wrapper will tear.) Fold the bottom edge of the wrapper over the filling and press to seal. Then fold the sides of the wrapper toward the center, tucking in the filling. Gently roll and firmly seal.

5. Repeat to use all of the remaining ingredients. Serve with the peanut sauce for dipping. Store individually wrapped in the refrigerator for 2 to 3 days.

MAKE IT WITH MEAT Slice cooked shrimp lengthwise and layer into the roll.

Nutrition per summer roll
Calories 178 | Total Fat 6g | Saturated Fat 1g | Cholesterol 0mg | Sodium 40mg |
Total Carbohydrate 25g | Dietary Fiber 4g | Sugars 1g | Protein 4g |

BAKED FETA
IN TOMATO LENTIL SAUCE

This crowd-pleasing appetizer is easy and perfect for a cozy evening. The hot, gooey feta and tangy, sweet tomato sauce will melt in your mouth, so scoop up every last drop with the baguette slices.

SERVES 4 ▪ PREP 15 MINS ▪ COOK 50 MINS

1 tbsp olive oil

1 garlic clove, minced

1 (28oz/830ml) can crushed tomatoes

2 tsp chopped oregano

1 tbsp balsamic vinegar

Pinch of red pepper flakes

½ cup cooked yellow lentils

Salt and pepper

8oz (226g) feta cheese block

1 baguette, cut into 1-in (2.5cm) slices, toasted

1. Heat the oven to 350°F (180°C). In a large saucepan, heat the oil over medium-low heat until hot. Add the garlic and cook for 2 to 3 minutes until soft but not browned.

2. Stir in the crushed tomatoes, oregano, vinegar, and red pepper flakes. Bring to a boil and add the lentils. Reduce to a simmer over medium-low heat and cook, covered, for 15 minutes or until the tomato sauce is warmed through. Taste and season with salt and pepper.

3. Transfer the tomato sauce to a 3-quart (3 liter) casserole or baking dish. Slice the feta into ½-inch (1cm) rounds or squares and arrange in an even layer on top of the sauce.

4. Bake, uncovered, for 12 minutes or until the feta is soft and slightly melted. Serve immediately with the baguette slices.

Nutrition per serving
Calories 330 | Total Fat 16g | Saturated Fat 9g | Cholesterol 50mg | Sodium 950mg |
Total Carbohydrate 34g | Dietary Fiber 8g | Sugars 12g | Protein 15g

BELUGA LENTIL & OLIVE TAPENADE

This olive spread from the Provence region of France is a flavorful make-ahead appetizer. Serve with a toasted baguette or crudités.

SERVES 6 ▪ PREP 5 MINS ▪ COOK 5 MINS

1 cup pitted Kalamata olives

1 cup cooked beluga lentils

2 garlic cloves

1½ tbsp drained capers

¼ cup olive oil

1. In a food processor, add the olives, lentils, garlic, and capers. Pulse to combine.

2. With the processor running on low, drizzle in the oil until the mixture is smooth. Serve immediately or store in an airtight container in the refrigerator for up to 3 days.

MAKE IT WITH MEAT For an extra briny punch, add 2 anchovy fillets to the mixture.

Nutrition per serving
Calories 220 | Total Fat 12g | Saturated Fat 1.5g | Cholesterol 0mg | Sodium 105mg |
Total Carbohydrate 23g | Dietary Fiber 6g | Sugars <1g | Protein 8g

LEMONY SPINACH HUMMUS

The bold green color of this citrusy hummus screams healthy. The fresh garnishes and bright flavor taste great with pita bread or as a spread for wraps and sandwiches.

SERVES 6 ▪ PREP 5 MINS ▪ COOK 5 MINS

1 cup cooked chickpeas,
  skins removed

4 cups baby spinach

2 garlic cloves

Juice and zest of 1 large lemon

1 tbsp tahini

¼ cup olive oil

Salt and pepper

1½ tbsp chia seeds, to garnish

Alfalfa sprouts, to garnish

Microgreens, to garnish

1. In a food processor, combine the chickpeas, spinach, garlic, lemon juice and zest, and tahini. Process on low for 1 minute to combine the ingredients.

2. With the processor on high, drizzle in the oil until smooth. For a thinner consistency, gradually add cold water, 1 tablespoon at a time, until the desired texture is achieved.

3. Transfer to a serving bowl and garnish with chia seeds, sprouts, and microgreens. Serve immediately.

MAKE IT WITH MEAT For a Middle Eastern appetizer, top with 8oz (250g) cooked ground lamb, spiced as desired.

Nutrition per serving
Calories 140 | Total Fat 10g | Saturated Fat 1.5g | Cholesterol 0mg | Sodium 20mg |
Total Carbohydrate 11g | Dietary Fiber 4g | Sugars 2g | Protein 4g |

SPICY CARROT HUMMUS

Harissa is a natural match for the sweetness of carrots and the tang of tahini in this hummus. Serve with crisp vegetables or seeded crackers.

SERVES 6 ▪ PREP 20 MINS ▪ COOK 30 MINS

¾lb (340g) carrots, ends trimmed (7–8 carrots)

¼ cup plus 1 tbsp olive oil, divided

2 cups cooked chickpeas, skins removed

1 tbsp water

1½ tbsp tahini

Juice of 1 large lime

1 tbsp harissa paste

Salt and pepper

1. Preheat the oven to 350°F (180°C). Peel the carrots and cut into 1-inch (3cm) pieces. Toss with 1 tablespoon oil and arrange in a single layer on a baking sheet. Roast for 25 to 30 minutes or until caramelized and tender. Remove from the oven and let cool.

2. In a food processor, combine the chickpeas with the water and pulse briefly to combine. Add the tahini, lime juice, harissa paste, and roasted carrots. With the processor running on low, drizzle in the remaining ¼ cup oil. Taste and season with salt and pepper, and then pulse a few more times to combine. Serve immediately.

Nutrition per serving
Calories 240 | Total Fat 16g | Saturated Fat 2g | Cholesterol 0mg | Sodium 250mg |
Total Carbohydrate 22g | Dietary Fiber 6g | Sugars 6g | Protein 6g |

RED LENTIL CAPONATA

Caponata is a sweet-and-sour Sicilian eggplant dish. Serve it as an appetizer with toasted baguette.

SERVES 6 ▪ PREP 25 MINS ▪ COOK 1 HR

1 large eggplant, cubed

3 tbsp olive oil, divided

1 medium yellow onion, diced

2 garlic cloves, minced

1 celery stalk, chopped

2 large tomatoes, deseeded and chopped

3 tbsp capers

2 tbsp toasted pine nuts

¼ cup golden raisins

½ cup cooked red lentils

1 tbsp granulated sugar

⅓ cup red wine vinegar

Pinch of red pepper flakes

Dash of ground cinnamon

Dash of unsweetened cocoa powder

Salt and pepper

1. Preheat the oven to 400°F (200°C). Spread the eggplant on a baking sheet. Drizzle with 2 tablespoons oil. Roast for 20 minutes or until tender.

2. In a large skillet, heat the remaining 1 tablespoon oil over medium heat until shimmering. Add the onion and cook for 5 to 10 minutes or until softened. Add the garlic and cook for 1 minute. Add the celery, tomatoes, and eggplant, and cook for 5 minutes.

3. Stir in the capers, pine nuts, raisins, lentils, sugar, vinegar, red pepper flakes, cinnamon, and cocoa powder. Simmer for 10 minutes, covered. Taste and season with salt and pepper. Remove from the heat and let cool. Refrigerate in an airtight container for 2 hours or overnight before serving. Serve cool or at room temperature.

Nutrition per serving
Calories 180 | Total Fat 11g | Saturated Fat 1.5g | Cholesterol 0mg | Sodium 500mg | Total Carbohydrate 22g | Dietary Fiber 6g | Sugars 12g | Protein 4g

RED PEPPER & WHITE BEAN DIP

This flavor-packed 15-minute dip is the ultimate recipe for easy entertaining.

SERVES 8 ▪ PREP 15 MINS

2 cups cooked chickpeas, skins removed

1½ cups roasted red peppers (drained)

2 cups cooked great northern beans

Zest and juice of 1 lemon

1 tsp red pepper flakes

1 tbsp thyme leaves

1 tbsp chopped flat-leaf parsley

1 tbsp olive oil

Salt and pepper

1. In a food processor, add the chickpeas, roasted red peppers, great northern beans, lemon zest and juice, red pepper flakes, thyme, and parsley. Purée on low speed until combined.

2. With the food processor running on low, drizzle in the oil. Taste and season with salt and pepper, and pulse to incorporate until smooth but not runny. Serve immediately with pita or crudité. Store in an airtight container in the refrigerator for up to 2 days.

Nutrition per serving
Calories 150 | Total Fat 3g | Saturated Fat 0g | Cholesterol 0mg | Sodium 400mg |
Total Carbohydrate 23g | Dietary Fiber 7g | Sugars 4g | Protein 8g

WHITE BEAN BUTTER
WITH RADISHES

Radishes with butter and salt are a classic French snack. Here, the butter is browned and blended with white beans to make a luxurious and creamy dip.

SERVES 4 ▪ PREP 5 MINS ▪ COOK 10 MINS

2 tbsp unsalted butter

1 cup cooked great northern beans

1 garlic clove

1 tsp water (optional)

1 bunch radishes, trimmed

Flaky sea salt

1. In a small saucepan, melt the butter over low heat. Cook until the butter takes on a light brown color and nutty aroma, and then immediately remove from the heat.

2. In a food processor, combine the butter, great northern beans, and garlic. Blend on high speed until smooth, adding up to 1 teaspoon water as needed to reach the desired consistency.

3. Transfer the white bean dip to a small bowl and serve alongside radishes and a small dish of flaky sea salt.

Nutrition per serving
Calories 110 | Total Fat 6g | Saturated Fat 3.5g | Cholesterol 15mg | Sodium 10mg |
Total Carbohydrate 10g | Dietary Fiber 3g | Sugars <1g | Protein 4g

MUNG BEAN GUACAMOLE

The addition of mung beans brings a nutritional boost and an extra creamy texture to this Mexican classic. Serve with tortilla chips or alongside your favorite tacos.

SERVES 2 ▪ PREP 20 MINS

2 large avocados

Juice of 1 lime

1 white onion, finely chopped

2 garlic cloves, minced

1 medium tomato, diced

½ cup cooked mung beans

2 tbsp roughly chopped cilantro

Salt and pepper

1. Cut the avocados in half, remove the pits, and scoop the flesh into a large bowl. Immediately add the lime juice. With a pastry cutter or fork, roughly mash the avocado.

2. Add the onion, garlic, tomato, mung beans, and cilantro. Gently stir to combine. Season with salt and pepper to taste. Serve immediately.

Nutrition per serving

Calories 300 | Total Fat 21g | Saturated Fat 3g | Cholesterol 0mg | Sodium 170mg |
Total Carbohydrate 25g | Dietary Fiber 15g | Sugars 4g | Protein 7g |

NAVY BEAN & ARTICHOKE PAN BAGNAT

This French sandwich is the ultimate picnic or packed lunch recipe. It gets better the longer it sits as the bread absorbs the vinaigrette and vegetable flavors.

MAKES 4 ▪ PREP 50 MINS

3 tbsp red wine vinegar

1½ tbsp olive oil

1 small cucumber, peeled, deseeded, and thinly sliced

1 small red onion, thinly sliced

1 (14oz/396g) can artichoke hearts (drained)

1 cup cooked navy beans

2 garlic cloves

½ cup cornichon pickles, drained

¼ cup flat-leaf parsley leaves

2 tbsp plain Greek yogurt

Pinch of red pepper flakes

Salt and pepper

1 whole wheat baguette

12 large basil leaves

1 Roma tomato, thinly sliced

2 hard-boiled eggs, thinly sliced

⅓ cup pitted Niçoise olives, roughly chopped

1. In a medium mixing bowl, combine the red wine vinegar, oil, cucumber, and red onion. Toss to combine and set aside to marinate while you prepare the rest of sandwich.

2. In a food processor, add the artichoke hearts, navy beans, garlic, cornichons, parsley, yogurt, and red pepper flakes. Pulse until combined but not smooth. Taste and season with salt and pepper.

3. Slice the baguette in half lengthwise to make a long sub. Lay the two halves cut-side up on the work surface. To make space for the filling, remove about a 1-inch (3cm) wide channel of bread from each side.

4. To assemble the sandwich, in the bottom half of the baguette arrange the basil leaves in a single layer. Top with the artichoke–navy bean mixture in an even layer. Then top with tomato and hard-boiled egg slices.

5. In the top half of the baguette, evenly spread the cucumber and red onion mixture. Drizzle on any remaining liquid. Top with Niçoise olives.

6. Carefully place the top half of the baguette atop the bottom half. Cut into 4 equal sandwiches. Wrap each with parchment paper and let marinate in the refrigerator for at least 30 minutes or overnight before serving.

MAKE IT VEGAN   Omit the egg and use a dairy-free yogurt substitute rather than Greek yogurt.

MAKE IT WITH MEAT   For more briny flavor, add 8 canned anchovy fillets along with the olives.

Nutrition per sandwich
Calories 320 | Total Fat 6g | Saturated Fat 1g | Cholesterol 0mg | Sodium 920mg |
Total Carbohydrate 52g | Dietary Fiber 11g | Sugars 6g | Protein 13g |

SUMAC ROASTED CHICKPEAS

Salty, tangy, and crispy, these roasted chickpeas are a healthy and addictive poppable snack.

SERVES 4 ▪ PREP 5 MINS ▪ COOK 1 HR

2 tbsp olive oil

Zest and juice of 2 lemons

2 tsp ground sumac

1 tsp kosher salt

4 cups cooked chickpeas, thoroughly drained and dried

1. Preheat the oven to 375°F (190°C). In a large mixing bowl, combine the oil, lemon zest and juice, sumac, and salt. Add the chickpeas and toss to coat thoroughly. Spread the chickpeas in an even layer on a baking sheet.

2. Bake for 40 to 45 minutes or until golden brown and lightly crispy, stirring every 10 to 15 minutes. Remove the baking sheet from the oven and place on a wire cooling rack. Let cool completely on the tray. Serve immediately or store in an airtight container on the counter for up to 3 days.

Nutrition per serving
Calories 330 | Total Fat 11g | Saturated Fat 1.5g | Cholesterol 0mg | Sodium 570mg |
Total Carbohydrate 47g | Dietary Fiber 13g | Sugars 8g | Protein 15g

QUINOA & MOTH BEAN DOLMADES

The distinct flavors of dill and mint combine with the textures of currants and pine nuts in these stuffed grape leaves. The flavors strengthen with time for a delicious make-ahead lunch.

MAKES 24 ▪ PREP 30 MINS ▪ COOK 1 HR

1 (8oz/227g) jar whole grape leaves

1 cup cooked quinoa

1½ tbsp chopped mint

1½ tbsp chopped dill

1½ tbsp chopped flat-leaf parsley

¼ cup dried currants

¼ cup toasted pine nuts

2 tbsp olive oil, divided

3 tbsp lemon juice, divided

Salt and pepper

1 cup cooked moth beans

1 cup vegetable stock

1. Preheat the oven to 350°F (180°C). Lightly coat a 9 x 13-inch (23 x 33cm) baking dish with cooking spray. Fill a large bowl with warm water. Soak the grape leaves for 2 to 3 minutes or until pliable. Drain into a colander. Cover the colander with a wet towel so the leaves remain moist.

2. To make the filling, in a large mixing bowl combine the quinoa, mint, dill, parsley, currants, pine nuts, 1 tablespoon oil, 1 tablespoon lemon juice, and cooked moth beans. Season with salt and pepper to taste.

3. Working one at a time to assemble the dolmades, place one grape leaf on a clean, flat work surface, vein-side up, and cut off the stem. Add 1 heaping tablespoon filling in the center, toward the bottom of the leaf. Fold the sides of the leaf over the filling and roll from the stem-end to the tip to make a tight roll. Place seam-side down in the baking dish. Repeat with the remaining leaves, arranging them snugly in the dish.

4. Pour the stock over the dolmades and drizzle on the remaining 1 tablespoon oil and the remaining 2 tablespoons lemon juice.

5. Cover the baking dish with aluminum foil and bake for 20 to 30 minutes or until all of the liquid is absorbed and the dolmades are moist and steaming. Serve immediately or let cool and store in the refrigerator in an airtight container for up to 2 days.

WHY NOT TRY... Sprinkle ⅓ cup finely crumbled feta cheese into the quinoa filling before rolling the dolmades.

Nutrition per dolma
Calories 60 | Total Fat 2.5g | Saturated Fat 0g | Cholesterol 0mg | Sodium 220mg |
Total Carbohydrate 7g | Dietary Fiber 2g | Sugars 2g | Protein 2g |

MASALA CHICKPEA NACHOS

This hybrid recipe combines the warm spices of Indian cuisine with the comfort and crunchiness of traditional Mexican nachos.

SERVES 6 ▪ PREP 40 MINS ▪ COOK 20 MINS

3 cups packed cilantro leaves, divided

1 cup mint leaves

2 tbsp lemon juice

¼ tsp ground ginger

⅓ cup plus 1 tbsp cold water, divided

Salt and pepper

2 cups cooked chickpeas

1 tsp curry powder

1 tsp garam masala

1 tbsp vegetable oil

10 papadum, cooked according to pkg instructions

2 cups shredded mozzarella cheese

½ cup mango chutney

¼ cup diced red onion

1 large lime, cut into 6 wedges

1. Prepare the cilantro-mint sauce. In a blender combine 2 cups cilantro, mint, lemon juice, ginger, and ⅓ cup water. Purée until smooth. Season with salt and pepper to taste. Transfer to an airtight container and set aside.

2. Preheat the oven to 400°F (200°C). Line a rimmed baking sheet with foil. Toss the chickpeas with the curry powder, garam masala, and oil. Spread in an even layer on the baking sheet and bake for 10 minutes or until slightly crispy and warmed through. Transfer the chickpeas to a bowl and wipe off the baking sheet.

3. Break each papadum into quarters and arrange in a single layer on the baking sheet. Sprinkle half of the mozzarella over the papadum and top with the chickpea mixture. Then top with the remaining mozzarella and bake for 10 to 12 minutes until the mozzarella melts and the papadum are lightly brown.

4. Meanwhile, in a small saucepan, heat the mango chutney with the remaining 1 tablespoon water. Cook for 2 to 3 minutes or until thin and warmed through.

5. To finish assembly, sprinkle the onion over the melted cheese. Drizzle the mango chutney sauce over the top. Dollop cilantro-mint sauce over the nachos. Chop the remaining 1 cup cilantro and sprinkle over the nachos. Garnish with the lime wedges and serve immediately, directly from the sheet.

MAKE IT WITH MEAT Layer 4½ ounces (130g) cooked shredded chicken with the chickpeas in step 3.

Nutrition per serving
Calories 420 | Total Fat 18g | Saturated Fat 12g | Cholesterol 40mg | Sodium 660mg |
Total Carbohydrate 40g | Dietary Fiber 6g | Sugars 13g | Protein 26g

EVERYTHING CHICKPEA FLOUR CRACKERS

Chickpea flour has a nutty flavor that pairs well with these everything bagel–inspired crackers. The crunchy seeds enhance the texture and go well with your favorite hummus or dip.

MAKES 24 ▪ PREP 30 MINS ▪ COOK 15 MINS

½ tbsp white sesame seeds

½ tbsp black sesame seeds

½ tbsp poppy seeds

½ tsp baking powder

1 cup chickpea flour

¾ tsp salt

⅛ tsp onion powder

⅛ tsp garlic powder

2 tbsp olive oil

¼ cup water, plus more to brush

1. Prepare the seed mixture. In a small bowl, stir together the white and black sesame seeds and poppy seeds. Set aside.

2. Preheat the oven to 375°F (190°C). Prepare a clean, flat work area and cut two large pieces of parchment paper of equal size, about 12 x 16-inches (31 x 41cm).

3. Make the dough. In a large mixing bowl, combine the baking powder, chickpea flour, salt, onion powder, garlic powder, and oil. Gradually incorporate ¼ cup water until the dough forms, adding additional water a spoonful at a time as needed, just until the dough is cohesive and pliable. Refrigerate for 10 minutes.

4. Divide the dough into two pieces and place side-by-side between the two sheets of parchment paper, about 5 inches (13cm) apart. With a rolling pin, roll out as thinly as possible into 2 rectangles, about ⅛ inch (3mm) thick.

5. Remove the top sheet of parchment paper. With a pizza cutter or paring knife, score the rolled dough into 1-inch (3cm) squares for 24 total crackers. Brush the dough with 1 to 2 teaspoons water, and then sprinkle the seed mixture evenly across the top.

6. Transfer the bottom piece of parchment paper directly onto a baking sheet. Bake for 10 to 15 minutes or until the edges start to brown and the crackers are firm. Remove from oven and place the second parchment sheet of unbaked crackers into the oven. Let the baked crackers rest at room temperature for 5 minutes, and then break the crackers apart. Store in an airtight container for up to 3 days.

Nutrition per cracker
Calories 30 | Total Fat 1.5g | Saturated Fat 0g | Cholesterol 0mg | Sodium 75mg |
Total Carbohydrate 2g | Dietary Fiber 0g | Sugars 0g | Protein 1g |

SOUPS & STEWS

TOMATILLO SOUP
WITH NAVY BEANS & CORN

Inspired by Mexican tortilla soup, this recipe has great texture from the corn and tang from the tomatillos. The creamy avocado and fresh cilantro garnish make this dish extra special.

SERVES 10 ▪ PREP 20 MINS ▪ COOK 55 MINS

2 tbsp vegetable oil

1 medium white onion, diced

2 large garlic cloves, minced

1 jalapeño, deseeded and finely diced

Pinch of red pepper flakes

15 medium tomatillos, about 1½ inches (4cm) in diameter, husked and roughly chopped

6 cups vegetable stock

Kernels from 2 white or yellow ears of corn

3½ cups cooked navy beans

Juice of 2 large limes

¼ cup chopped cilantro

Salt and pepper

Cubes of ripe avocado, to serve

Lime wedges, to serve

1. In a large stockpot or soup pot, heat the oil over medium heat until shimmering. Add the onion and cook for 5 to 10 minutes until translucent but not brown. Add the garlic, jalapeño, and red pepper flakes, and cook for 2 minutes or until soft.

2. Stir in the tomatillos. Cook for 7 to 8 minutes, covered, or until the tomatillos begin to soften. Stir in the stock and bring the mixture to a boil. Reduce the heat and simmer, covered, for 20 to 25 minutes.

3. Stir in the corn, navy beans, lime juice, and cilantro. Cook for another 8 to 10 minutes to heat the ingredients through. Taste and season with salt and pepper. Serve immediately with cubed avocado and limes wedges.

MAKE IT WITH MEAT Add 5 ounces (140g) cooked and shredded chicken when you stir in the corn and white beans.

WHY NOT TRY... For chewy texture, add ½ cup hominy along with the corn, and reduce the navy beans to 3 cups.

Nutrition per serving
Calories 330 | Total Fat 8g | Saturated Fat 1.5g | Cholesterol 0mg | Sodium 115mg |
Total Carbohydrate 55g | Dietary Fiber 15g | Sugars 6g | Protein 11g

HOPPIN' JOHN SOUP

Traditionally served in the South on New Year's Day to bring good luck, Hoppin' John soup is usually a side dish. Here it's transformed into a hearty and healthy meal.

SERVES 6 ▪ PREP 30 MINS ▪ COOK 45 MINS

1 tbsp olive oil

1 small yellow onion, diced

1 small red bell pepper, deseeded and diced

2 celery stalks, diced

1 garlic clove, minced

1 (14.5oz/411g) can diced tomatoes (undrained)

2 thyme sprigs

Pinch of cayenne

½ tsp smoked paprika

4 cups vegetable stock

Salt and pepper

2 cups cooked black-eyed peas

1½ cups cooked brown rice

½ cup chopped green onion

¼ cup chopped flat-leaf parsley

1. In a large saucepan, warm the oil over medium heat until shimmering. Add the onion and cook for 5 to 10 minutes or until it starts to become translucent. Add the bell pepper and celery and cook for an additional 2 minutes. Add the garlic and cook for an additional minute.

2. Stir in the tomatoes, thyme, cayenne, paprika, and stock. Bring to a boil and then reduce the heat to low. Cook at a simmer, covered, for 20 minutes. Taste and season with salt and pepper.

3. Stir in the black-eyed peas and rice. Cook for an additional 10 minutes or until the black-eyed peas and rice are warmed through. Serve immediately garnished with green onion and parsley.

MAKE IT WITH MEAT Stir in 5 ounces (140g) cooked, chopped, and smoked turkey leg or ham when adding the stock and tomatoes.

Nutrition per serving
Calories 180 | Total Fat 3g | Saturated Fat 0g | Cholesterol 0mg | Sodium 680mg |
Total Carbohydrate 30g | Dietary Fiber 6g | Sugars 5g | Protein 6g

LIMA BEAN BISQUE

The natural creaminess of lima beans gives this soup the texture of a bisque without the heavy cream. Serve with homemade croutons and freshly cracked black pepper.

SERVES 4 ▪ PREP 15 MINS ▪ COOK 35 MINS

1 tbsp unsalted butter

1 medium yellow onion, chopped

2 celery stalks, chopped

4 cups cooked lima beans

5 cups vegetable stock

½ tsp red pepper flakes

4 thyme sprigs

2 tbsp chopped basil

2 tbsp chopped flat-leaf parsley

Salt and pepper

1. In a large stockpot, melt the butter over medium heat. Add the onion and cook for 5 to 10 minutes or until it starts to become translucent but not browned. Add the celery and cook for an additional 3 to 4 minutes or until it starts to soften.

2. Add the lima beans and stir to combine. Pour in the stock and bring to a boil. Add the red pepper flakes and thyme, and then reduce the heat to low. Simmer, uncovered, for 15 minutes. Turn off the heat, remove the thyme stems, and stir in the basil and parsley. Let cool slightly.

3. With a high-powered blender or immersion blender, purée the soup until completely smooth. (If using a blender, you may have to work in batches.) Reheat the soup in the pot. Season with salt and pepper to taste. Serve immediately.

MAKE IT WITH MEAT Garnish each bowl with 1 tablespoon crispy crumbled bacon or prosciutto.

Nutrition per serving
Calories 280 | Total Fat 3.5g | Saturated Fat 2g | Cholesterol 10mg | Sodium 190mg |
Total Carbohydrate 46g | Dietary Fiber 15g | Sugars 10g | Protein 15g |

GUMBO Z'HERBES

Also known as green gumbo, Gumbo Z'herbes is a longstanding tradition in Louisiana. The classically vegetarian soup is often eaten on Good Friday and thought to bring good luck all year long.

SERVES 10 ▪ PREP 1 HR 10 MINS ▪ COOK 1 HR

1 bunch Swiss chard

1 bunch kale

1 bunch watercress

1 bunch mustard greens

1 bunch dandelion greens

2 cups baby spinach

6 cups water

1½ cups cooked moth beans, divided

⅔ cup vegetable oil

⅔ cup all-purpose flour

1 medium yellow onion, diced

1 medium green bell pepper, diced

3 celery stalks, diced

1 garlic clove, minced

2 cups vegetable stock

2 bay leaves

½ tsp paprika

3 thyme sprigs

1 tsp cayenne

2 tbsp white wine vinegar

Salt and pepper

Hot sauce (optional), to serve

1. Remove and discard the tough stems and ribs from the Swiss chard, kale, watercress, mustard greens, dandelion greens, and spinach leaves. You want approximately 2 pounds (1kg) total. Roughly chop the greens and place in a large bowl. Cover with cold water. Agitate to release dirt or grit. Drain.

2. In a stockpot, bring the 6 cups water to a rolling boil. Add the greens and cook, covered, for 15 to 20 minutes or until tender. Reserve 2 cups cooking liquid, and drain the cooked greens.

3. In a blender or food processor, blend together half of the cooked greens, ¾ cup moth beans, and the reserved cooking liquid until smooth. Set aside.

4. To make the roux, in a large heavy-bottomed stockpot or Dutch oven, heat the oil over medium heat. Once shimmering, add the flour and stir until smooth. Reduce the heat to low and stir continuously for 10 to 15 minutes or until the roux is the color of peanut butter and the consistency of milk.

5. Immediately stir in the onion, bell pepper, and celery. Cook for 2 to 3 minutes over medium heat, stirring continuously, until the mixture thickens and the vegetables are coated. Add the garlic, stock, bay leaves, paprika, thyme, and cayenne. Pour in the puréed greens and moth bean mixture and cook, covered, for 15 minutes.

6. Add the remaining cooked greens and moth beans and briskly simmer for 15 minutes, covered. Stir in the vinegar. Taste and season with salt and pepper. Remove the bay leaf and thyme stems. Serve immediately with hot sauce (if using).

MAKE IT WITH MEAT Add 5 ounces (140g) shredded or chopped smoked turkey.

Nutrition per serving
Calories 260 | Total Fat 16g | Saturated Fat 10g | Cholesterol 0mg | Sodium 390mg |
Total Carbohydrate 25g | Dietary Fiber 8g | Sugars 4g | Protein 8g

MUNG BEAN GREEN GAZPACHO

Green gazpacho is a unique spin on the classic Spanish cold soup. It's best served ice cold, so don't skimp on the refrigeration time.

SERVES 4 ▪ PREP 30 MINS

2 cups packed arugula

1 medium cucumber, peeled, deseeded, and chopped

1 garlic clove

¾ cup cooked mung beans

¼ cup roughly chopped cilantro

¼ cup mint leaves

3 green onions, chopped

1 avocado, halved, peeled, and pitted

1 tbsp olive oil

2 tsp red wine vinegar

Juice of 1 large lemon

1¼ cups cold water

Salt and pepper

2 tbsp chopped chives

¼ cup sprouted mung beans

1. In a food processor, combine the arugula, cucumber, garlic, mung beans, cilantro, mint, and green onion. Blend on high speed until finely chopped.

2. Add the avocado, oil, vinegar, and lemon juice. Process on high speed while slowly pouring in the cold water. Taste and season with salt and pepper and pulse once more to combine.

3. Transfer to an airtight container and refrigerate for at least 2 hours or until chilled. Portion the gazpacho into four serving bowls and garnish each with ½ tablespoon chopped chives and 1 tablespoon sprouted mung beans. Serve cold.

MAKE IT WITH MEAT Sauté 1 pound (450g) peeled and deveined shrimp and garlic, and add atop each bowl before serving.

WHY NOT TRY... Garnish each serving with 1 tablespoon diced avocado and a drizzle of extra virgin olive oil.

Nutrition per serving
Calories 180 | Total Fat 12g | Saturated Fat 2g | Cholesterol 0mg | Sodium 580mg |
Total Carbohydrate 17g | Dietary Fiber 8g | Sugars 5g | Protein 6g |

KABOCHA SQUASH & YELLOW LENTIL SOUP

Kabocha is a winter squash with a sweet flavor and vivid orange flesh. Roasting enhances its sweetness, making it a natural companion to curry and coconut milk.

SERVES 4 ▪ PREP 20 MINS ▪ COOK 1 HR 45 MINS

1 medium kabocha squash, deseeded and cut into quarters (skin on)

2 tbsp olive oil, divided

1 carrot, chopped

1 yellow onion, chopped

1 celery stalk, chopped

5 cups vegetable broth, divided

1½ cups dried yellow lentils

2 tsp curry powder

½ tsp ground ginger

1 (5.6fl oz/165ml) can full-fat unsweetened coconut milk

Salt and pepper

1 medium lime, cut into 4 wedges

Unsweetened toasted coconut flakes, to garnish

1. Preheat the oven to 350°F (180°C). Place the squash quarters cut-side up on a baking sheet and drizzle with 1 tablespoon oil. Roast for 40 minutes, or until tender. Let cool.

2. Meanwhile, in a stockpot, heat the remaining 1 tablespoon oil over medium heat. Add the carrot, onion, and celery and cook for 5 to 10 minutes or until the onion is translucent.

3. Add 3 cups broth and the yellow lentils and bring to a boil. Reduce to a simmer and cook, covered, for 45 to 60 minutes or until the lentils are tender. To ensure there is enough liquid for the lentils to absorb, add up to 2 cups additional broth as needed.

4. When the lentils are tender, scoop the roasted kabocha away from skin and add the flesh to the pot. Stir in the curry powder and ginger and heat through. With a blender or immersion blender, purée until smooth. Stir in the coconut milk and heat thoroughly. Season with salt and pepper to taste. Serve with a lime wedge and coconut flakes.

Nutrition per serving
Calories 322 | Total Fat 15g | Saturated Fat 8g | Cholesterol 0mg | Sodium 287mg |
Total Carbohydrate 41g | Dietary Fiber 13g | Sugars 4g | Protein 8g |

MUNG BEAN & MISO NOODLE SOUP

This comforting traditional Asian soup gets an extra layer of texture and a boost of protein with the addition of mung beans.

SERVES 6 ▪ PREP 15 MINS ▪ COOK 15 MINS

5 cups low-sodium vegetable broth

3 tbsp white miso paste

1 tbsp grated ginger

2 garlic cloves, minced

2 tbsp rice wine vinegar

2 tsp soy sauce

3oz (85g) dried Japanese udon noodles

1½ cups cooked mung beans

7oz (200g; about ½ block) extra firm tofu, drained, pressed, and cubed

2 cups shredded Napa or Savoy cabbage

½ cup sliced green onion, to garnish

1. In a Dutch oven or stockpot, stir together the broth, miso paste, ginger, garlic, vinegar, and soy sauce.

2. Bring the mixture to a boil and add the udon noodles. Reduce the heat and simmer for 5 to 6 minutes or until the udon start to become tender.

3. Add the mung beans, tofu, and cabbage. Stir to combine and cook for 5 minutes or until the udon are completely cooked and the tofu is warmed through.

4. Transfer to serving bowls and garnish with green onion. Serve immediately.

MAKE IT WITH MEAT For a seafood version, add ½ pound (225g) cooked peeled and deveined shrimp to the broth along with the mung beans.

Nutrition per serving
Calories 160 | Total Fat 3g | Saturated Fat 0g | Cholesterol 0mg | Sodium 630mg |
Total Carbohydrate 24g | Dietary Fiber 6g | Sugars 5g | Protein 11g |

GREEN MINESTRONE
WITH ARUGULA PESTO

Minestrone is a classic Italian soup of vegetables and beans. This one uses the fresh green produce of springtime and is topped off with a dollop of vibrant homemade pesto.

SERVES 6 ▪ PREP 50 MINS ▪ COOK 40 MINS

½ cup plus 1 tbsp olive oil, divided

1 large leek, white and light green parts sliced and rinsed

1 large celery stalk, diced

1 garlic clove, minced

5 cups vegetable stock

1 bay leaf

1 thyme sprig

Pinch of red pepper flakes

2 cups cooked navy beans

1 small zucchini, diced

1 cup trimmed and cut green beans (1-in/3cm pieces)

1 tbsp chopped basil

1 cup frozen green peas, thawed

1 cup shredded savoy cabbage

½ tsp chopped oregano

Salt and pepper

1 cup baby arugula

½ cup pine nuts, toasted

1 cup grated Parmesan cheese

1 tsp grated lemon zest

1. In a medium stockpot, heat 1 tablespoon oil over medium heat. Add the white and light green parts of the leek and cook for 5 minutes or until it begins to soften. Add the celery and garlic and cook for an additional 2 to 3 minutes.

2. Add the stock, bay leaf, thyme, red pepper flakes, and navy beans. Bring to a boil and then reduce the heat and simmer, covered, for 15 minutes or until the navy beans are warmed through.

3. Add the zucchini, green beans, basil, green peas, savoy cabbage, and oregano. Simmer for an additional 15 minutes or until the vegetables are tender and cooked through. Taste and season with salt and pepper.

4. While the soup is simmering, make the pesto. In a food processor, combine the arugula, pine nuts, Parmesan, and lemon zest. With the processor running, slowly drizzle in the remaining ½ cup oil until fully combined.

5. Remove the bay leaf and thyme stem from the soup. Serve immediately with a dollop or swirl of the pesto.

MAKE IT WITH MEAT Add 5 ounces (140g) cooked cubed chicken along with the vegetables in step 3.

Nutrition per serving
Calories 390 | Total Fat 20g | Saturated Fat 5g | Cholesterol 10mg | Sodium 410mg | Total Carbohydrate 30g | Dietary Fiber 11g | Sugars 5g | Protein 15g |

CARIBBEAN BLACK BEAN & LENTIL SOUP

Bell peppers and jalapeño flavor this comforting and slightly spicy soup, made heartier with black beans and beluga lentils.

SERVES 4 ▪ PREP 25 MINS, PLUS 8 HRS FOR SOAKING ▪ COOK 30 MINS

1 tbsp vegetable oil

1 cup yellow onion, diced

½ cup red bell pepper, diced

½ cup green bell pepper, diced

1 small jalapeño, deseeded and minced

1 tbsp garlic, minced

4 cups vegetable stock

1 bay leaf

2 cups dried black beans, presoaked for at least 8 hours, rinsed and drained

1 cup cooked Beluga lentils

1½ tsp allspice

¼ tsp cayenne

½ tsp smoked paprika

Juice of 2 medium limes

Salt and pepper

Chopped cilantro, to garnish

1. In a medium stockpot or Dutch oven, heat the oil over medium heat until shimmering. Add the onion, red bell pepper, green bell pepper, and jalapeño. Cook for 5 to 10 minutes or until the vegetables begin to soften. Add the garlic and cook for an additional 1 to 2 minutes.

2. Stir in the stock, bay leaf, soaked black beans, Beluga lentils, allspice, cayenne, and paprika. Bring to a boil and then reduce the heat and simmer, covered, for 20 minutes or until the soup begins to thicken.

3. Stir in the lime juice. Taste and season with salt and pepper. Remove the bay leaf and garnish with cilantro before serving.

MAKE IT WITH MEAT For a natural addition of meat, add 1 (3–4oz; 84–110g) cooked and crumbled or sliced smoked sausage along with vegetables in step 1.

Nutrition per serving
Calories 400 | Total Fat 7g | Saturated Fat 3g | Cholesterol 0mg | Sodium 150mg |
Total Carbohydrate 68g | Dietary Fiber 17g | Sugars 7g | Protein 21g |

YELLOW LENTIL MULLIGATAWNY

This spicy and sweet lentil soup is an Anglo-Indian classic.

SERVES 8 ▪ PREP 25 MINS ▪ COOK 50 MINS

2 tbsp coconut oil

1 medium yellow onion, diced

2 celery stalks, diced

2 carrots, diced

3 garlic cloves, minced

¾ tsp curry powder

¾ tsp ground coriander

¼ tsp cayenne

1 cup dried yellow lentils

1 (14oz/411g) can crushed tomatoes

4 cups vegetable broth

1 (13.5fl oz/400ml) can full-fat unsweetened coconut milk

Juice of 2 large limes

Salt and pepper

Chopped cilantro, to garnish

1. In a stockpot, heat the coconut oil over medium heat until shimmering. Add the onion, celery, and carrots, and cook for 5 to 10 minutes or until softened. Add the garlic and cook for an additional minute.

2. Add the curry powder, coriander, and cayenne. Cook for 1 minute, and then stir in the lentils. Add the crushed tomatoes, broth, and coconut milk. Bring to a boil and then reduce the heat and simmer, covered, for 20 to 35 minutes or until the lentils are tender.

3. Stir in the lime juice. Taste and season with salt and pepper. Transfer to serving bowls, garnish with cilantro, and serve immediately.

Nutrition per serving

Calories 200 | Total Fat 9g | Saturated Fat 7g | Cholesterol 0mg | Sodium 190mg | Total Carbohydrate 24g | Dietary Fiber 6g | Sugars 6g | Protein 7g |

PIGEON PEA &PUMPKIN CHILI

Pumpkin may seem like an unusual ingredient in chili, but its sweetness is a lovely complement to this soup's spice.

SERVES 6 ▪ PREP 25 MINS ▪ COOK 50 MINS

1 tbsp olive oil

1 small yellow onion, diced

2 garlic cloves, minced

1 small jalapeño, deseeded and minced

1 (14oz/411g) can diced tomatoes (undrained)

2½ tsp ground cumin

1½ tsp chipotle chili powder

2 cups vegetable stock

2½ cups cooked pigeon peas

2 cups cooked adzuki beans

1 cup corn kernels

1 (15oz/425g) can 100 percent pure pumpkin

Salt and pepper

¾ cup chopped cilantro, to garnish

1. In a large stockpot, heat the oil over medium heat until shimmering. Add the onion and cook for 5 to 10 minutes or until softened. Add the garlic and jalapeño and cook for an additional minute.

2. Stir in the diced tomatoes, cumin, and chipotle chili powder. Stir in the stock, bring to a boil, and then reduce the heat and simmer, uncovered, for 5 minutes. Stir in the pigeon peas, adzuki beans, and corn. Bring to a boil and then reduce the heat to low and simmer, covered, for an additional 20 minutes.

3. Stir in the pumpkin. Cook, covered, for an additional 10 minutes. Taste and season with salt and pepper. Transfer to serving bowls, garnish with cilantro, and serve immediately.

MAKE IT WITH MEAT Cook ½ pound (225g) ground turkey along with the onion in step 1.

Nutrition per serving
Calories 360 | Total Fat 4g | Saturated Fat 0.5g | Cholesterol 0mg | Sodium 180mg |
Total Carbohydrate 68g | Dietary Fiber 16g | Sugars 9g | Protein 15g |

CHICKPEA & NAVY BEAN BISQUE

While not a traditional bisque, this soup certainly seems like one with its silky, rich texture. This simple, elegant recipe makes an excellent first course for a dinner party.

SERVES 4 ▪ PREP 15 MINS ▪ COOK 30 MINS

½ tbsp olive oil, plus extra to garnish

1 leek (white parts only), sliced and rinsed

1 garlic clove, minced

1 tbsp dry vermouth

3 cups vegetable stock

2 cups cooked navy beans

1 cup cooked chickpeas

¼ cup heavy cream

Salt and pepper

Chopped toasted hazelnuts, to garnish

1. In a Dutch oven or large pot, warm the oil over medium heat until shimmering. Add the leek and cook for 4 to 5 minutes until soft and translucent. Add the garlic and cook for an additional 2 minutes.

2. Stir in the vermouth and cook for 1 to 2 minutes. Incorporate the stock, navy beans, and chickpeas. Bring to a boil and then reduce the heat and simmer, covered, for 15 minutes. Remove from the heat and let cool slightly.

3. With a high-powered blender or immersion blender, purée the soup until completely smooth. (If using a blender, you may have to work in batches.) Return to the pot over medium heat, stir in the heavy cream, and heat. Taste and season with salt and pepper. Transfer to serving bowls, garnish with hazelnuts and a swirl of oil, and serve immediately.

Nutrition per serving
Calories 270 | Total Fat 6g | Saturated Fat 2g | Cholesterol 10mg | Sodium 390mg |
Total Carbohydrate 41g | Dietary Fiber 14g | Sugars 5g | Protein 12g

PIGEON PEA, QUINOA & KALE SOUP

This soup is hearty and filling without being heavy. It's also a nutritional powerhouse with a trifecta of superfood ingredients providing vitamins, fiber, and protein.

SERVES 4 ▪ PREP 25 MINS ▪ COOK 50 MINS

1 tbsp olive oil

1 small yellow onion, diced

1 large carrot, diced

1 celery stalk, diced

1 garlic clove, minced

Pinch of red pepper flakes

Leaves of 3 thyme sprigs

1 bay leaf

7 cups vegetable stock

1 (14.5oz/411g) can diced
   tomatoes (undrained)

1 cup dried tri-color quinoa

2 cups cooked pigeon peas

2 cups chopped kale

Salt and pepper

1. In a Dutch oven or stockpot, warm the oil over medium heat until shimmering. Add the onion, carrot, and celery, and cook for 5 to 10 minutes or until tender but not brown. Add the garlic and cook for an additional minute.

2. Add the red pepper flakes, thyme leaves, and bay leaf. Stir to combine and cook for 1 minute. Stir in the stock and diced tomatoes. Bring to a boil, and then add the quinoa. Reduce the heat to low and cook, partially covered, for 25 minutes or until the quinoa is cooked.

3. Stir in the pigeon peas and kale. Cook for an additional 10 minutes or until the kale is tender. Taste and season with salt and pepper. Remove the bay leaf and serve immediately.

MAKE IT WITH MEAT Remove the casings from 2 links mild Italian sausage. Crumble and brown alongside the garlic.

Nutrition per serving

Calories 380 | Total Fat 7g | Saturated Fat 0.5g | Cholesterol 0mg | Sodium 740mg |
Total Carbohydrate 67g | Dietary Fiber 15g | Sugars 14g | Protein 15g

SOUTHWEST NAVY BEAN SOUP

This soup has the vivid flavors of chili, lime, and cilantro, with a light, brothy texture.

SERVES 6 ▪ PREP 10 MINS, PLUS 8 HRS FOR SOAKING ▪ COOK 1 HR 10 MINS

1 tbsp olive oil

1 medium yellow onion, diced

1 small jalapeño, deseeded and diced

1 garlic clove, minced

4½ cups vegetable stock

1 tsp ground cumin

1 tsp smoked paprika

1 tsp dried oregano leaves

1 tsp ancho chili powder

3 cups navy beans, presoaked for at least 8 hours, rinsed and drained

Juice of 1 lime

1 tbsp chopped cilantro

Salt and pepper

1. In a stockpot, heat the oil over medium heat until shimmering. Add the onion and jalapeño and cook for 5 to 10 minutes or until softened. Add the garlic and cook for an additional minute.

2. Stir in the stock, cumin, paprika, oregano, and chili powder. Add the navy beans and stir to combine. Bring to a boil and then reduce the heat and simmer, covered, for 45 to 60 minutes or until the beans are completely tender.

3. In a blender, purée ¾ cup soup until smooth. Return to the pot and stir to combine.

4. Stir in the lime juice and cilantro. Taste and season with salt and pepper. Serve immediately.

MAKE IT WITH MEAT Ham naturally complements navy beans. Add 2 ounces (55g) chopped cooked ham along with the beans.

Nutrition per serving
Calories 280 | Total Fat 3.5g | Saturated Fat 0g | Cholesterol 0mg | Sodium 290mg | Total Carbohydrate 47g | Dietary Fiber 18g | Sugars 5g | Protein 16g

SMOKY TOMATO & SPLIT PEA BISQUE

Smoky chipotle and fire-roasted tomatoes flavor this creamy soup.

SERVES 6 ▪ PREP 25 MINS ▪ COOK 50 MINS

1 tbsp olive oil

1 medium yellow onion, chopped

1 carrot, diced

1 celery stalk, diced

1 garlic clove, minced

1 (14.5oz/411g) can fire-roasted chopped tomatoes (undrained)

3 cups cooked yellow split peas

1 chipotle in adobo sauce, minced

3 cups vegetable stock

1 tsp ground coriander

Juice of 1 medium lime

⅓ cup heavy cream

Salt and pepper

1. In a medium stockpot or Dutch oven, heat the oil over medium heat until shimmering. Add the onion, carrot, and celery, and cook for 5 to 10 minutes or until starting to soften. Add the garlic and cook for 1 to 2 minutes.

2. Stir in the fire-roasted tomatoes, split peas, chipotle, stock, and coriander. Bring to a boil and then reduce the heat and simmer, covered, for 20 to 25 minutes or until the soup thickens. Remove from the heat and let cool slightly.

3. With a high-powered blender or immersion blender, purée the soup until completely smooth. (If using a blender, you may have to work in batches.) Return the soup to the pot and reheat.

4. Stir in the lime juice and heavy cream. Season with salt and pepper and serve immediately.

MAKE IT VEGAN Instead of heavy cream, use an equal amount of coconut cream.

Nutrition per serving
Calories 230 | Total Fat 8g | Saturated Fat 3.5g | Cholesterol 20mg | Sodium 380mg |
Total Carbohydrate 32g | Dietary Fiber 11g | Sugars 8g | Protein 9g

CREAMY SPINACH & MUNG BEAN SOUP

This soup is everything you love about creamed spinach. Don't let the bright color fool you—it's as rich as it is good for you, so sop it up with freshly baked bread.

SERVES 4 ▪ PREP 25 MINS ▪ COOK 40 MINS

1 tbsp unsalted butter

1 medium yellow onion, diced

1 garlic clove, minced

1 medium russet potato, peeled and cut into ½-inch (1cm) chunks

3 cups vegetable broth, divided

6oz (170g) baby spinach

1 cup cooked mung beans

2 tbsp dry sherry

⅛ tsp cayenne

⅛ tsp ground nutmeg

Salt and pepper

¼ cup grated Parmesan cheese

1. In a Dutch oven or stockpot, melt the butter over medium heat. Add the onion and cook for 5 to 10 minutes or until translucent. Add the garlic and cook for an additional minute.

2. Stir in the potato and cook for 2 to 3 minutes. Add 2 cups broth and bring to a boil. Reduce the heat to a simmer and cook, covered, for 12 to 15 minutes or until the potatoes are fork-tender.

3. Add the spinach and mung beans and cook for an additional 5 minutes or until the spinach wilts and the mung beans are warmed through. Let cool slightly.

4. With a high-powered blender or immersion blender, purée the soup until completely smooth. (If using a blender, you may have to work in batches.) Return the puréed mixture to the pot and stir in the sherry, cayenne, and nutmeg. For a thinner consistency, add up to 1 cup remaining broth. Taste and season with salt and pepper.

5. Reheat the soup over medium heat. Transfer to serving bowls and top with Parmesan. Serve immediately.

MAKE IT VEGAN Replace the butter with an equal amount coconut oil.

WHY NOT TRY... Garnish with flat-leaf parsley or watercress for more pronounced green flavor.

Nutrition per serving
Calories 180 | Total Fat 5g | Saturated Fat 3g | Cholesterol 15mg | Sodium 800mg |
Total Carbohydrate 25g | Dietary Fiber 6g | Sugars 4g | Protein 8g

PINTO BEAN PEANUT STEW

Peanut soups and stews are a staple in areas of Africa. This unusual dish combines creamy peanut butter with beans and bitter greens for a hearty meal.

SERVES 6 ▪ PREP 25 MINS ▪ COOK 50 MINS

1 tbsp coconut oil

1 small yellow onion, chopped

1 garlic clove, minced

1 large sweet potato, peeled and cut into 1-in (3cm) cubes

1 tsp ancho chili powder

½ tsp cayenne

1 (14.5oz/411g) can crushed tomatoes

2½ cups vegetable broth

½ cup creamy peanut butter

3 cups cooked pinto beans

3 cups chopped mustard greens

Salt and pepper

Chopped cilantro, to garnish

1. In a medium stockpot, heat the coconut oil over medium heat until shimmering. Add the onion and cook for 5 to 10 minutes or until softened. Add the garlic and cook for 1 minute.

2. Add the sweet potato, ancho chili powder, and cayenne. Stir to combine. Pour in the crushed tomatoes and broth. Bring to a boil and then reduce the heat and simmer, uncovered, for 5 minutes.

3. Stir in the peanut butter. Return to a boil and then reduce the heat and simmer, covered, for 10 minutes.

4. Fold in the pinto beans and mustard greens. Return to a boil once more, and then reduce the heat and simmer, covered, for 15 minutes or until the mustard greens are tender. Taste and season with salt and pepper. Garnish with cilantro and serve immediately.

MAKE IT WITH MEAT Add 7 ounces (200g) raw smoked andouille sausage, diced, along with the onion in step 1.

Nutrition per serving
Calories 330 | Total Fat 14g | Saturated Fat 4.5g | Cholesterol 0mg | Sodium 220mg |
Total Carbohydrate 40g | Dietary Fiber 13g | Sugars 8g | Protein 16g |

SALADS & SIDES

SWEET POTATO & BELUGA LENTIL SALAD
DRESSED WITH HONEY & LEMON

The nuttiness and slight tooth of the lentils mixed with the soft, caramelized sweet potato is a wonderful play of flavors and textures.

SERVES 2 ▪ PREP 25 MINS, PLUS COOLING ▪ COOK 45 MINS

1 large sweet potato, peeled and cubed

Dash of smoked paprika

2 tbsp olive oil, divided

Salt and pepper

3 cups water

1½ cups dried beluga lentils

2 green onions, thinly sliced

1 large celery stalk, diced; leafy tops reserved for garnish

¼ cup crumbled feta cheese

1 tbsp honey or agave nectar, slightly warmed

Juice of 1 medium lemon

1. Preheat the oven to 350°F (180°C). On a rimmed baking sheet, toss the sweet potato with the paprika and 1 tablespoon oil. Spread evenly and season with salt and pepper to taste. Roast until tender and slightly caramelized, about 25 minutes, stirring once halfway through. Let cool to room temperature.

2. Meanwhile, in a medium pot, bring the 3 cups water to a boil. Add the lentils and return to a boil for 2 to 3 minutes. Reduce the heat and simmer, covered, for 25 to 30 minutes or until tender but not soft. Drain in a fine mesh colander and let cool to room temperature.

3. Assemble the salad. In a large mixing bowl, combine the lentils, sweet potatoes, onion, celery, and feta. Mix well. Drizzle in the honey, lemon juice, and remaining 1 tablespoon oil. Toss to combine. Taste and season with salt and pepper. Garnish with the reserved celery leaves and serve at room temperature.

MAKE IT VEGAN Use a nut-based vegan cheese alternative rather than feta.

Nutrition per serving
Calories 480 | Total Fat 19g | Saturated Fat 5g | Cholesterol 15mg | Sodium 1380mg | Total Carbohydrate 63g | Dietary Fiber 11g | Sugars 16g | Protein 17g |

THREE BEAN SALAD STUFFED AVOCADOS

These stuffed avocados are filled with the Southwest flavors of corn and cilantro. They are a beautiful presentation. The three beans are a protein dream and the avocado is a wonderful source of healthy fats.

SERVES 8 ▪ PREP 20 MINS ▪ COOK 15 MINS

1 yellow or white ear of corn

½ cup cooked black beans

½ cup cooked pigeon peas

½ cup cooked mung beans or sprouted mung beans

½ cup cooked farro

1 orange or yellow bell pepper, diced

3 tbsp sour cream

¼ tsp smoked paprika

½ tsp ground cumin

1 tsp red wine vinegar

Juice of 2 medium limes

1 tbsp olive oil

Salt and pepper

4 ripe avocados

½ cup chopped cilantro

1. On a grill or using a gas burner, char the ear of corn for 1 to 2 minutes per side or until the kernels are slightly blackened. Let cool slightly.

2. In a large mixing bowl, combine the black beans, pigeon peas, mung beans, farro, and bell pepper. Carefully slice the kernels from the cob and stir into the mixture.

3. Make the dressing. In a small bowl, whisk together sour cream, paprika, cumin, vinegar, and lime juice. Drizzle in the olive oil and whisk to combine thoroughly.

4. Pour the dressing over the bean mixture and toss to coat. Season with salt and pepper to taste.

5. Cut each avocado in half lengthwise and remove the pits. Mound an equal amount of the bean mixture into center of each avocado. Garnish with cilantro and serve.

Nutrition per serving
Calories 310 | Total Fat 18g | Saturated Fat 3.5g | Cholesterol 0mg | Sodium 300mg |
Total Carbohydrate 34g | Dietary Fiber 12g | Sugars 5g | Protein 8g

LARB CABBAGE CUPS
WITH SPROUTS & TOFU

Crisp cabbage cups are the perfect vessel for the bold umami-packed flavors of larb. Sprouted lentils and mung beans add a unique twist to this vegetarian version of the classic Thai dish.

MAKES 8 ▪ PREP 30 MINS ▪ COOK 20 MINS

Juice of 3 large limes

2 tbsp rice wine vinegar

2 garlic cloves, minced

1 tsp grated ginger

2 tbsp soy sauce

2 Thai chiles, deseeded and finely minced

12oz (340g) extra firm tofu, drained

2½ tbsp sesame oil

1 cup sprouted brown lentils

1 cup sprouted mung beans

⅓ cup chopped mint

⅓ cup chopped cilantro

8 small leaves Savoy cabbage or iceberg lettuce

½ cup chopped, roasted, unsalted peanuts

1. Make the dressing. In a large mixing bowl, whisk together the lime juice, vinegar, garlic, ginger, soy sauce, and chiles. Set aside.

2. With a paper towel, blot the tofu to absorb moisture, and then roughly chop. In a medium skillet, warm the sesame oil over medium heat. Add the tofu. With a spatula or wooden spoon, break into small crumbles. Cook for 10 to 12 minutes or until dry and lightly browned.

3. In the large mixing bowl, toss the tofu and dressing. Add the sprouted lentils, sprouted mung beans, mint, and cilantro. Stir to combine. Add about ½ cup tofu mixture into each cabbage leaf. Garnish with a sprinkle of chopped peanuts and serve immediately.

MAKE IT WITH MEAT For a more traditional larb, replace the tofu with ¾ pound (340g) cooked ground chicken or duck.

Nutrition per cabbage cup

Calories 180 | Total Fat 11g | Saturated Fat 1.5g | Cholesterol 0mg | Sodium 280mg | Total Carbohydrate 12g | Dietary Fiber 5g | Sugars 4g | Protein 9g |

BLACK GRAM & KALE SALAD
WITH MISO TAHINI DRESSING

Loaded with texture, this salad is unlike most green salads. The chewy kale, crunchy coconut, creamy beans, and tangy dressing are a dynamic combination.

SERVES 6 ▪ PREP 35 MINS

3 tbsp tahini

1½ tbsp miso paste

Juice of 1 large lime

1 tsp soy sauce

2 tsp honey

2 tbsp rice wine vinegar

¼ tsp red pepper flakes

¼ cup cold water

1 bunch kale, tough stems removed, leaves roughly chopped (about 6 cups)

1 cup unsweetened shredded coconut, toasted

1 cup cooked black gram

Salt and pepper

1. Make the dressing. In a small bowl, combine the tahini, miso paste, lime juice, soy sauce, honey, rice wine vinegar, and red pepper flakes. Add the water and whisk until smooth.

2. In a large salad bowl, add the chopped kale and about ¾ cup dressing. With your hands, massage the dressing into the kale for 1 to 2 minutes until the kale tenderizes slightly.

3. Add the toasted coconut and black gram and toss to combine. Season with salt and pepper to taste. Serve immediately.

MAKE IT WITH MEAT To transform this salad into an entrée, add 3 ounces (85g) cooked sliced chicken breast to each portion.

Nutrition per serving
Calories 210 | Total Fat 13g | Saturated Fat 8g | Cholesterol 0mg | Sodium 370mg |
Total Carbohydrate 19g | Dietary Fiber 7g | Sugars 5g | Protein 8g |

MOTH BEANS & GRILLED ROMAINE
WITH RED PEPPER VINAIGRETTE

Grilled lettuce may seem unusual, but it adds a deliciously faint smoky flavor and a layer of depth to green salads.

SERVES 6 ▪ PREP 20 MINS ▪ COOK 20 MINS

1 cup roasted red bell peppers (drained)

1 large garlic clove

1 tbsp red wine vinegar

½ tsp chopped oregano

1 tsp chopped basil

3 tbsp olive oil, divided

Salt and pepper

3 Romaine lettuce hearts

⅔ cup cooked moth beans

4oz (110g) soft goat cheese

1. In a food processor, combine the roasted peppers, garlic, vinegar, oregano, and basil. With the processor running, drizzle in 2 tablespoons oil. Taste and season with salt and pepper.

2. Carefully cut each Romaine heart in half lengthwise, leaving as much of the core intact as possible. Drizzle the lettuce with the remaining 1 tablespoon oil. On a grill or preheated grill pan, cook the Romaine halves for 1 to 3 minutes on each side or until slightly wilted and charred but not cooked through.

3. Arrange the grilled lettuce on a large serving platter. Scatter moth beans evenly across the top. Crumble goat cheese over the moth beans. Top with the dressing to taste. Garnish with freshly ground black pepper and serve immediately.

MAKE IT VEGAN Omit the goat cheese and substitute a tangy nut-based cheese alternative.

WHY NOT TRY... For an extra briny kick, garnish the salad with 3 to 4 tablespoons capers.

Nutrition per serving
Calories 200 | Total Fat 13g | Saturated Fat 5g | Cholesterol 15mg | Sodium 390mg |
Total Carbohydrate 14g | Dietary Fiber 7g | Sugars 4g | Protein 9g |

MUNG BEAN GADO GADO

Gado Gado is an Indonesian chopped salad whose name means "mix mix." It's always served with spicy peanut dressing, and here is accompanied by crisp vegetables and legumes.

SERVES 4 ▪ PREP 45 MINS

½ cup creamy peanut butter

1 tsp garlic powder

1½ tsp ground ginger

1 tsp red pepper flakes

1½ tsp soy sauce

Juice of 2 limes

1 tsp rice wine vinegar

¾ cup water

1 small beet, peeled

2 cups shredded Savoy cabbage

½ cup cooked mung beans

½ cup halved cherry tomatoes

½ cup sprouted mung beans

½ cup chopped green beans, blanched and drained

2 hard boiled eggs, quartered

1. Make the spicy peanut dressing. In a small bowl, whisk together the peanut butter, garlic powder, ginger, red pepper flakes, soy sauce, lime juice, and vinegar. Whisk in the water until thoroughly mixed. Set aside.

2. Using a spiralizer or mandoline, slice the beet into thin strips.

3. Assemble the salad on a large serving platter. Spread the cabbage in an even layer. In separate piles atop the cabbage, arrange the cooked mung beans, cherry tomatoes, sprouted mung beans, spiralized beet, green beans, and hard-boiled eggs. Serve immediately with the dressing on the side.

MAKE IT VEGAN Replace the hard-boiled egg with 1 cup cubed and seared tempeh or tofu.

MAKE IT WITH MEAT On the serving platter, include 6 ounces (170g) thinly sliced pan-seared steak.

Nutrition per serving
Calories 360 | Total Fat 24g | Saturated Fat 0g | Cholesterol 255mg | Sodium 390mg |
Total Carbohydrate 21g | Dietary Fiber 21g | Sugars 8g | Protein 21g |

CHICKPEA & CHERRY SALAD

This salad combines the flavors of summertime in a single bowl. The tart sweetness of the cherries mixes with the nuttiness of the chickpeas to create an unusual side dish.

SERVES 4 ▪ PREP 15 MINS

3 tbsp apple cider vinegar

1 tbsp olive oil

1 tsp honey

2 cups cooked chickpeas

1 cup dark-sweet cherries, pitted and halved

2 tbsp chopped basil

1½oz (40g) ricotta salata cheese, crumbled

Salt and pepper

1. Make the dressing. In a small bowl, whisk together the vinegar, oil, and honey. Set aside.

2. In a large salad bowl, add the chickpeas and cherries. Add the basil and mix thoroughly. Drizzle the dressing over the mixture and toss to evenly coat.

3. Top with crumbled ricotta salata. Taste and season with salt and pepper and serve immediately.

MAKE IT VEGAN Omit the ricotta salata and use ¼ cup capers for added brininess.

Nutrition per serving
Calories 220 | Total Fat 8g | Saturated Fat 2.5g | Cholesterol 10mg | Sodium 380mg |
Total Carbohydrate 30g | Dietary Fiber 8g | Sugars 10g | Protein 9g

LENTIL & CAULIFLOWER TABBOULEH

Using cauliflower to make "rice" is an easy hack that adds nutrition without sacrificing flavor. Here, it works beautifully with fresh mint and herbs in this Middle Eastern salad.

SERVES 8 ▪ PREP 25 MINS

1 small head of cauliflower

1 cup chopped flat-leaf parsley

1 cup chopped curly parsley

1 cup diced seedless cucumber

1 cup diced tomato

1 small bunch green onions, thinly sliced

1 cup cooked brown lentils

½ cup chopped mint

Zest and juice of 2 lemons

2 tbsp olive oil

Salt and pepper

1. Remove the outer leaves from the cauliflower head and break into florets. Place in a food processor and pulse 6 to 7 times or until the cauliflower resembles rice or bulgar.

2. In a large mixing bowl, combine the riced cauliflower, flat-leaf parsley, curly parsley, cucumber, tomato, green onion, lentils, and mint. Add the lemon zest and juice and olive oil, and toss to combine. Taste and season with salt and pepper. Transfer to a serving dish and serve immediately.

MAKE IT WITH MEAT Top each serving with 3 ounces (85g) grilled steak slices.

Nutrition per serving
Calories 83 | Total Fat 4g | Saturated Fat 0.5g | Cholesterol 0mg | Sodium 310mg | Total Carbohydrate 11g | Dietary Fiber 3g | Sugars 2g | Protein 4g

LIMA BEAN PANZANELLA

Panzanella is a Tuscan bread salad that is quite popular in the warmer months. It's a great use for day-old bread and wonderful for parties and potlucks because you can serve it at room temperature.

SERVES 6 ▪ PREP 25 MINS ▪ COOK 15 MINS

1 small loaf sourdough bread

¼ cup red wine vinegar

1 tbsp Dijon mustard

½ cup olive oil

2 garlic cloves, minced

1 tsp chopped oregano

1 tsp chopped basil

1 cup halved cherry tomatoes

1½ cups cooked lima beans

1 English cucumber, diced

1 cup fresh yellow corn kernels

Salt and pepper

1. Preheat the oven to 325°F (170°C). Cut the bread into ½-inch (1cm) cubes to make about 4 cups. On a baking sheet, arrange the cubed bread in a single layer and bake for 15 minutes or until toasted and lightly golden brown.

2. Meanwhile, make the dressing. In a small bowl, whisk together the vinegar and Dijon mustard. While whisking, drizzle in the oil and thoroughly combine. Stir in the garlic, oregano, and basil.

3. To assemble, in a large mixing bowl, add the tomatoes, lima beans, cucumber, and corn. Fold in the toasted bread, then drizzle the vinaigrette over the mixture. Toss to coat. Taste and season with salt and pepper. Serve immediately.

Nutrition per serving
Calories 430 | Total Fat 12g | Saturated Fat 2g | Cholesterol 0mg | Sodium 380mg |
Total Carbohydrate 69g | Dietary Fiber 9g | Sugars 5g | Protein 14g

ROASTED CARROTS & CHICKPEAS
WITH VADOUVAN YOGURT

Vadouvan is a curry spice blend originating from Southern India. Cool yogurt tempers the spice and pairs well with the sweetness of roasted carrots.

SERVES 4 ▪ PREP 15 MINS ▪ COOK 30 MINS

1lb (450g) whole young carrots, leafy tops chopped and reserved for garnish

2 tbsp olive oil

2 cups cooked chickpeas

2 tsp red wine vinegar

1 garlic clove, minced

1 tsp thyme leaves

Pinch of red pepper flakes

Salt and pepper

¾ cup plain Greek yogurt

1 tbsp vadouvan spice blend

1. Preheat the oven to 350°F (150°C). Arrange the carrots in a single layer on a rimmed baking sheet and drizzle with the olive oil. Roast for 25 to 30 minutes or until fork-tender.

2. Meanwhile, in a separate small mixing bowl, toss together the chickpeas, vinegar, garlic, thyme, and red pepper flakes. Taste and season with salt and pepper. Set aside.

3. In a small mixing bowl, stir together the Greek yogurt and vadouvan.

4. Spread the yogurt on a serving platter, arrange the roasted carrots over the yogurt, and top with the chickpea mixture. Garnish with freshly ground black pepper and the reserved carrot tops. Serve immediately.

MAKE IT VEGAN Substitute plain soy yogurt rather than Greek yogurt.

Nutrition per serving
Calories 270 | Total Fat 9g | Saturated Fat 1.5g | Cholesterol <5mg | Sodium 230mg |
Total Carbohydrate 37g | Dietary Fiber 7g | Sugars 12g | Protein 11g |

ROASTED TOMATOES & WHITE BEANS
WITH BASIL VINAIGRETTE

Roasted tomatoes are lush and flavorful. Here they combine with a fresh and healthful green vinaigrette for a tasty side.

SERVES 4 ▪ PREP 15 MINS ▪ COOK 30 MINS

4 Roma tomatoes

2 garlic cloves, minced

3 tbsp extra virgin olive oil, divided

1½ cups basil leaves, plus more to garnish

¼ cup white wine or champagne vinegar

Salt and pepper

2 cups cooked great northern beans

1. Preheat the oven to 400°F (200°C). Cut the tomatoes in half lengthwise. Place on a rimmed baking sheet and toss with the garlic and 1 tablespoon oil. Roast for 30 minutes. Let cool to room temperature.

2. Meanwhile, make the basil vinaigrette. In a blender or food processor, process the basil and vinegar. Running on low speed, drizzle in the remaining 2 tablespoons oil until emulsified. Taste and season with salt and pepper.

3. In a separate mixing bowl, toss the great northern beans with 2 tablespoons dressing and spread on a serving platter. Arrange the roasted tomatoes on top. Season with salt and pepper to taste. Top with any remaining dressing and basil leaves. Serve immediately.

Nutrition per serving
Calories 214 | Total Fat 10g | Saturated Fat 1.5g | Cholesterol 0mg | Sodium 591mg |
Total Carbohydrate 22g | Dietary Fiber 7g | Sugars 1.7g | Protein 8.5g

PATTIES & TACOS

MUNG BEAN BURGERS
WITH RED CURRY SAUCE

This textured veggie burger includes mung beans
to give the patty great bite and a lovely green color.

MAKES 6 ▪ PREP 25 MINS ▪ COOK 25 MINS

1 shallot, finely minced

1 garlic clove, finely minced

2 cups cooked mung beans

¼ tsp ground coriander

Pinch of red pepper flakes

2 tbsp chopped cilantro

1 tbsp chopped mint

2 large eggs, beaten

⅓ cup panko breadcrumbs

Salt and pepper

½ cup plain Greek yogurt

½ tbsp red curry paste

6 hamburger buns or small pitas

Alfalfa sprouts, for topping

1. Preheat the oven to 375°F (190°C). Line a baking sheet with parchment paper or spray with cooking spray. In a large mixing bowl, combine the shallot, garlic, mung beans, coriander, red pepper flakes, cilantro, and mint. With a pastry cutter or the back of a fork, lightly mash the mixture, keeping about half of the mung beans intact.

2. Add the eggs and stir to mix thoroughly. Gently fold in the breadcrumbs and season with salt and pepper.

3. With a measuring cup, portion out ½ cup packed mung bean mixture. Invert onto the baking sheet and lightly flatten to make a patty. Repeat to make 6 patties total. Bake the patties for 20 minutes, gently flipping them halfway through the cooking time.

4. Meanwhile, make the red curry sauce. In a small mixing bowl, whisk together the yogurt and red curry paste. Taste and season with salt and pepper.

5. Assemble each burger with a generous smear of the sauce, a patty, and alfalfa sprouts. Serve immediately.

MAKE IT VEGAN Mix 2 tablespoons flax seeds with 6 tablespoons water to replace each egg. Instead of Greek yogurt, use plain coconut yogurt.

Nutrition per burger
Calories 360 | Total Fat 17g | Saturated Fat 3g | Cholesterol 70mg | Sodium 400mg |
Total Carbohydrate 37g | Dietary Fiber 5g | Sugars 5g | Protein 13g

BLACK-EYED PEA SLIDERS
WITH PICO DE GALLO

*The pico de gallo on these sliders adds wonderful texture
and moisture to the creamy black-eyed pea patties.*

MAKES 8 ▪ PREP 30 MINS ▪ COOK 20 MINS

1 tbsp plus 1 tsp olive oil, divided

1 small yellow onion, diced

1 garlic clove, minced

2 small jalapeños, deseeded and diced (about 3 tbsp), divided

½ tsp chipotle chili powder

2½ tsp ground cumin

2½ cups cooked black-eyed peas

2 large eggs, beaten

⅓ cup panko breadcrumbs

1 large tomato, deseeded and diced

1 small white onion, diced

¼ cup chopped cilantro

Juice of 1 large lime

8 slider buns

1. Preheat the oven to 300°F (150°C). In a large nonstick skillet, heat 2 teaspoons oil over medium heat until shimmering. Add the yellow onion and cook for 5 to 10 minutes or until softened. Stir in the garlic and half of the jalapeño. Cook for 2 minutes. Transfer the mixture to a large mixing bowl and set aside. Set aside the skillet, leaving any residual oil.

2. To the vegetable mixture, add the chipotle chili powder, cumin, black-eyed peas, eggs, and breadcrumbs. With a potato masher, mix to combine and slightly break up the black-eyed peas.

3. Return the skillet to the stove and heat over medium heat. Working in batches, make 8 patties total, adding more oil to the skillet as needed. Portion out ⅓ cup bean mixture and use your hands to form into a patty. Cook in the skillet for 3 to 4 minutes on each side, pressing lightly with a spatula to sear. Transfer the patties to a baking sheet. Transfer the sheet to the oven and bake for 8 to 10 minutes or until the patties are cooked through.

4. Meanwhile, make pico de gallo. In a small bowl, combine the tomato, onion, remaining jalapeño, cilantro, and lime.

5. Assemble the sliders with a patty and 1 tablespoon each of pico de gallo. Serve immediately.

MAKE IT WITH MEAT To add smokiness, finely dice one slice bacon and cook along with the garlic and jalapeño in step 1.

Nutrition per slider
Calories 230 | Total Fat 6g | Saturated Fat 1g | Cholesterol 75mg | Sodium 290mg | Total Carbohydrate 34g | Dietary Fiber 5g | Sugars 4g | Protein 9g

INDIAN POTATO & CHICKPEA PATTIES

The golden hue and warm Indian spices in these patties are reminiscent of masala dosa, a traditional potato-stuffed pancake. Serve these alongside chutney and raita.

MAKES 14 ▪ PREP 25 MINS ▪ COOK 1 HR

4½ cups peeled and diced yukon gold potatoes (7–8 potatoes)

1½ cups cooked chickpeas

3 tbsp ghee, divided

1 small red onion, finely diced

1 garlic clove, minced

1½ tsp garam masala

1 tsp ground ginger

¾ tsp ground coriander

½ cup green peas

½ cup panko breadcrumbs

Salt and pepper

¼ cup chopped cilantro, for garnish

1. Bring a large stockpot full of water to a boil. Add the potatoes and cook for 20 minutes or until fork-tender. Drain and let dry in a colander for 15 minutes.

2. In a large mixing bowl, with a potato masher, roughly mash the chickpeas. Add the potatoes and mash again to combine.

3. In a medium nonstick skillet, heat 1 tablespoon ghee over medium heat. Add the onion and cook for 5 to 10 minutes or until softened. Add the garlic and cook for an additional minute. Stir in the garam masala, ginger, and coriander. Cook for an additional minute to warm the spices.

4. In the mixing bowl, combine the onion mixture with the potato-chickpea mixture. Add the remaining 2 tablespoons ghee and stir to combine. Stir in the green peas and breadcrumbs. Mix thoroughly. Taste and season with salt and pepper.

5. Working in batches, portion out a ⅓ cup mixture and form into a patty with your hands. In the nonstick skillet, cook the patties over medium heat for 4 to 5 minutes on each side or until warmed through and lightly golden brown. Garnish the patties with cilantro and serve immediately.

MAKE IT VEGAN Instead of ghee, use any light oil such as canola or vegetable.

WHY NOT TRY... For heat, cook one small green chile, deseeded and minced, with the garlic and onion.

Nutrition per patty
Calories 100 | Total Fat 4g | Saturated Fat 2g | Cholesterol 5g | Sodium 15g |
Total Carbohydrate 13g | Dietary Fiber 3g | Sugars 2g | Protein 3g

PIGEON PEA PATTIES
WITH GUAVA SAUCE

These patties have all of the spice found in Jamaican jerk seasoning balanced with the sweet heat of the guava glaze.

MAKES 10 ▪ PREP 30 MINS ▪ COOK 50 MINS

½ cup guava jelly

2 tbsp red wine vinegar

¼ tsp red pepper flakes

2 tbsp vegetable oil or canola oil, divided

1 small red onion, finely diced

1 Serrano chile, deseeded and minced

1 garlic clove, minced

½ tsp ground cinnamon

1 tsp ground cumin

¾ tsp ground nutmeg

1¼ tsp allspice

¼ tsp cayenne

3 cups cooked pigeon peas, divided

⅓ cup panko breadcrumbs

2 large eggs, beaten

3 tbsp chopped cilantro, to garnish

1. To make the guava sauce, in a small saucepan, combine the guava jelly, red wine vinegar, and red pepper flakes. Simmer over low heat for 8 to 10 minutes or until the jelly melts and the mixture is syrupy. Lower the heat and keep warm.

2. Meanwhile, in a medium skillet, heat 1 tablespoon oil over medium heat until shimmering. Add the onion and cook for 5 to 10 minutes or until softened. Add the Serrano chile and garlic and cook for an additional 1 to 2 minutes. Add the cinnamon, cumin, nutmeg, allspice, cayenne, and 2½ cups pigeon peas. Stir to combine.

3. Transfer the pigeon pea mixture to a food processor. Pulse until combined and slightly puréed. Transfer to a large mixing bowl and add the breadcrumbs, eggs, and remaining ½ cup whole pigeon peas. Fold together to combine.

4. Wipe out the medium skillet and return to the stove. Heat the remaining 1 tablespoon oil over medium heat. Working in batches and adding more oil to the skillet as needed, portion out ¼ cup pigeon pea mixture and place in the skillet, slightly flattening with a spatula. Cook for 3 to 4 minutes on each side or until golden brown.

5. Serve the patties immediately with the warm guava sauce.

MAKE IT VEGAN Instead of eggs, use ½ cup ripe avocado.

Nutrition per patty
Calories 180 | Total Fat 4g | Saturated Fat 0.5g | Cholesterol 35g | Sodium 20g |
Total Carbohydrate 26g | Dietary Fiber 4g | Sugars 9g | Protein 5g

SPIRALIZED BEET & KIDNEY BEAN PATTIES

The hot pink color and texture from the beet is truly special. Serve as you would your favorite veggie burger or alongside grilled chicken or pork.

MAKES 8 ▪ PREP 15 MINS ▪ COOK 30 MINS

2 medium red beets, peeled

2 cups cooked kidney beans

1 tbsp chopped green onion

1 tbsp chopped cilantro

Pinch of red pepper flakes

½ cup panko breadcrumbs

2 large eggs, beaten

Salt and pepper

1. Preheat the oven to 325°F (170°C). Line a baking sheet with parchment paper.

2. Using a spiralizer or mandoline, slice the beets into thin strips. (This should yield about 3 cups.) With kitchen shears, cut the strands into about 1-inch (3cm) pieces.

3. In a large mixing bowl, gently mash the kidney beans with a fork or pastry cutter, keeping some beans intact. Fold in the spiralized beets, green onion, cilantro, red pepper flakes, breadcrumbs, and eggs. Season with salt and pepper to taste.

4. Heat a large nonstick skillet over medium heat. Form the beet mixture into 8 equal patties. Working in batches as needed, cook the patties for 3 to 4 minutes on each side or until browned and holding together. Arrange on the baking sheet.

5. Bake the patties for 8 to 10 minutes or until cooked through. Serve immediately.

MAKE IT VEGAN Replace the eggs with an extra ½ cup cooked kidney beans and 2 tablespoons water, puréed in a food processor, and add to mixture in step 3.

Nutrition per patty

Calories 100 | Total Fat 1.5g | Saturated Fat 0g | Cholesterol 45mg | Sodium 330mg | Total Carbohydrate 16g | Dietary Fiber 4g | Sugars 2g | Protein 6g

RAINBOW LENTIL MEATBALLS
WITH ARRABIATTA SAUCE

Lentil meatballs and spicy tomato sauce are a healthy alternative to the comfort food classic, loaded with protein and fiber. Serve with pasta or bread and Parmesan cheese.

MAKES 18 ▪ PREP 15 MINS ▪ COOK 40 MINS

1½ cups cooked red lentils, thoroughly drained

⅔ cup cooked brown lentils, thoroughly drained

1 large egg, lightly beaten

½ cup panko breadcrumbs

½ tsp garlic powder

1 tsp dried oregano

Zest of 1 large lemon

¼ tsp cayenne

2 tbsp olive oil

1 small yellow onion, minced

1 (28oz/800g) can crushed tomatoes

1 tbsp red pepper flakes

Salt and pepper

1. Preheat the oven to 350°F (180°C). Spray a baking sheet with cooking spray. In a large mixing bowl, combine the red lentils, brown lentils, egg, breadcrumbs, garlic powder, oregano, lemon zest, and cayenne.

2. With your hands, form the lentil mixture into about 1-tablespoon meatballs to make about 18 total. Place on the baking sheet. Bake for 25 minutes, rotating the meatballs halfway through.

3. Meanwhile, make the arrabiatta sauce. In a saucepan, heat the oil over medium heat until shimmering. Add the onion and cook for 5 to 10 minutes or until softened. Add the crushed tomatoes and red pepper flakes. Simmer over low heat for 15 minutes or until the sauce is warmed through. Season with salt and pepper to taste.

4. Serve the meatballs immediately with arrabiatta sauce.

MAKE IT WITH MEAT Add ½ pound (225g) ground beef or crumbled Italian sausage to the sauce along with the onion in step 3.

Nutrition per meatball
Calories 70 | Total Fat 2g | Saturated Fat 0g | Cholesterol 0mg | Sodium 115mg | Total Carbohydrate 9g | Dietary Fiber 2g | Sugars 2g | Protein 3g

ZUCCHINI & LIMA BEAN FRITTERS

These fritters are light and refreshing thanks to the lovely green color and burst of lemon zest. Serve as a side dish to grilled meats or top them with a poached egg and watercress.

MAKES 12 ▪ PREP 20 MINS ▪ COOK 30 MINS

4 medium zucchini

1 tbsp salt

1½ cups cooked lima beans

¼ tsp cayenne

2 tsp chopped basil

Zest of 1 large lemon

2 large eggs, beaten

¾ cup panko breadcrumbs

Salt and pepper

1 tbsp olive oil

1. With the wide side of a box grater, grate the zucchini. Place in a piece of cheesecloth or a thin kitchen towel and sprinkle with the salt. Squeeze to remove as much water as possible from the zucchini.

2. In a food processor or blender, combine the lima beans, cayenne, basil, lemon zest, and eggs. Blend on low speed for 30 to 45 seconds or until smooth. Transfer to a large mixing bowl and add the zucchini and breadcrumbs. Season with salt and pepper to taste. Stir to combine thoroughly.

3. In a nonstick skillet, heat the oil over medium heat. Working in batches and adding more oil as needed, portion out ¼ cup lima bean–zucchini mixture per fritter, gently form into a ball, and place into the skillet. With a spatula, lightly press down to form a patty. Cook for 2 to 3 minutes on each side or until lightly browned. Serve immediately.

MAKE IT VEGAN Use 6 tablespoons water and 2 tablespoons ground flax seeds, combined, to replace the egg.

Nutrition per patty
Calories 60 | Total Fat 1g | Saturated Fat 0g | Cholesterol 30mg | Sodium 220mg | Total Carbohydrate 10g | Dietary Fiber 2g | Sugars 2g | Protein 4g

BAKED FALAFEL
WITH PICKLED RED ONIONS
& SAMBAL OELEK

This falafel is oven-baked instead of fried for a healthier spin on this classic Middle Eastern street food. Pickled onions and sambal oelek are the perfect tangy, sweet, and spicy condiments.

MAKES 16 ▪ PREP 30 MINS, PLUS 3 HRS TO PICKLE ▪ COOK 40 MINS

1 cup apple cider vinegar

½ cup red wine vinegar

2 tbsp granulated sugar

1 tsp salt

1 large red onion, thinly sliced

1 garlic clove

2 cups cooked chickpeas

½ tsp baking soda

½ tsp ground coriander

½ tsp ground cumin

Pinch of red pepper flakes

1 bunch curly parsley, chopped

½ cup finely chopped cilantro

Zest and juice of 1 lemon

¼ cup chickpea flour

1 tbsp olive oil

Salt and pepper

¼ cup sambal oelek

1. Make the pickled red onions. In a medium saucepan, bring the apple cider vinegar, red wine vinegar, sugar, and salt to a boil over medium heat. Stir until the sugar and salt are dissolved. Remove from the heat. Add the red onion and stir to combine. Let cool completely at room temperature, stirring occasionally. Pour into a glass jar and secure with a lid. Refrigerate for 3 hours or overnight.

2. Preheat the oven to 400°F (200°C). In a food processor, combine the garlic, chickpeas, baking soda, coriander, cumin, red pepper flakes, parsley, cilantro, and lemon zest and juice. Pulse until combined but still crumbly.

3. Transfer the chickpea mixture to a medium mixing bowl. Fold in the chickpea flour. Drizzle the oil over the mixture and stir once more until holding together. Season with salt and pepper to taste.

4. Portion out approximately 2 tablespoons chickpea mixture and roll into a ball. Place on a baking sheet and repeat with the remaining mixture. With a spatula, slightly flatten each ball to form patties. Bake for 10 minutes, flip, and bake for an additional 10 minutes. Serve immediately with the pickled red onions and sambal oelek on side.

WHY NOT TRY... If you'd rather skip the heat, serve with tzatziki sauce instead of spicy sambal.

Nutrition per patty
Calories 60 | Total Fat 1.5g | Saturated Fat 0g | Cholesterol 0mg | Sodium 270mg |
Total Carbohydrate 9g | Dietary Fiber 2g | Sugars 2g | Protein 2g

BLACK-EYED PEA & COLLARD GREEN TACOS

Black-eyed peas and greens are a classic pairing. Here, with some creamy goat cheese and a splash of hot sauce, they make a unique taco filling.

MAKES 12 ▪ PREP 20 MINS ▪ COOK 40 MINS

1 tbsp olive oil

1 small yellow onion, finely diced

1 garlic clove, minced

5 cups packed collard greens (rinsed and roughly chopped)

2 cups vegetable stock

½ tsp white wine vinegar

⅛ tsp cayenne

2 cups cooked black-eyed peas

Salt and pepper

12 white or yellow corn tortillas

6oz (170g) goat cheese

Hot sauce (optional), to serve

1. In a medium Dutch oven or heavy-bottomed pot, heat the oil over medium heat until shimmering. Add the onion and cook for 5 to 10 minutes or until softened. Add the garlic and cook for an additional minute.

2. Stir in the collard greens. Add the stock, vinegar, and cayenne. Bring to a boil and then reduce the heat and simmer, covered, for 20 minutes or until the greens are tender. Add the black-eyed peas and cook for an additional 10 minutes or until the beans are warmed through and most of liquid has evaporated. Taste and season with salt and pepper.

3. Warm the tortillas in a skillet or char lightly on the burner of a stove. Assemble about 12 tacos with about ⅓ cup beans and greens mixture each (drained slightly with a slotted spoon), about 1 tablespoon goat cheese each, and a few dashes of hot sauce (if using). Roll up the tacos and serve immediately.

MAKE IT WITH MEAT Add 2½ ounces (70g) cooked smoked turkey or pork, chopped, along with the greens in step 2.

WHY NOT TRY... Add a spoonful of your favorite salsa to each taco.

Nutrition per taco
Calories 120 | Total Fat 4.5g | Saturated Fat 2g | Cholesterol 5mg | Sodium 110mg |
Total Carbohydrate 16g | Dietary Fiber 4g | Sugars 1g | Protein 6g

BEAN FLAUTAS
WITH AVOCADO CREMA

Meaty Scarlet Runner beans and cheese fill these baked flautas, Spanish for "flute."

MAKES 16 ▪ PREP 20 MINS ▪ COOK 10 MINS

1 cup sour cream

1 medium avocado, halved and pitted

Juice of 1 lime

1 cup cooked Scarlet Runner beans

1 cup grated sharp Cheddar cheese

4oz (110g) goat cheese

½ cup chopped green onion

½ cup fresh corn kernels

⅓ cup chopped cilantro

1 tbsp ground cumin

1 tsp cayenne

Salt

16 small flour tortillas

1. Preheat the oven to 400°F (200°C). Set up a wire cooling rack on a rimmed baking sheet.

2. To make the crema, in a food processor or blender, combine the sour cream, avocado, and lime juice until smooth. Refrigerate in a small bowl until ready to serve.

3. In a large mixing bowl, lightly mash the Scarlet Runner beans with a potato masher. Incorporate the Cheddar, goat cheese, green onion, corn, cilantro, cumin, and cayenne. Taste and season with salt.

4. To assemble, at one edge of a tortilla, place 2 tablespoons filling. Tightly roll, leaving the ends open. Place seam-side down on the wire rack. Repeat to make 16 flautas total. Bake for 20 minutes or until the edges are lightly browned. Serve immediately with crema on the side.

MAKE IT WITH MEAT Add 5 ounces (140g) cooked shredded chicken or beef to the filling when you add the cheese. This will yield at least 20 flautas.

Nutrition per flauta
Calories 210 | Total Fat 8g | Saturated Fat 4g | Cholesterol 10mg | Sodium 440mg | Total Carbohydrate 25g | Dietary Fiber 3g | Sugars 1g | Protein 10g

SPICED LENTIL TACOS
WITH GRILLED PINEAPPLE SALSA

Grilling the pineapple in this salsa enhances its already intense sweetness and balances the heat from the jalapeño.

MAKES 8 ▪ PREP 20 MINS ▪ COOK 45 MINS

1 cup dried brown lentils

2½ cups vegetable stock

1 bay leaf

Dash of garlic powder

¼ tsp ground ginger

½ tsp allspice

1½ tsp ground cumin

12oz (340g) fresh pineapple slices

1 small jalapeño, deseeded and finely diced

1 small white onion, diced

½ cup chopped cilantro

Juice of 1 lime

Salt and pepper

8 small corn tortillas

1. In a medium pot, stir together the lentils, stock, bay leaf, garlic powder, ground ginger, allspice, and cumin. Bring to a boil and then reduce the heat to medium-low and simmer, covered, for 30 to 35 minutes or until the lentils are tender and most of stock has been absorbed. Add water as needed. Remove the bay leaf and let sit, covered.

2. Meanwhile, heat a grill or grill pan over medium-high heat. Grill the pineapple slices for 2 to 3 minutes on each side or until caramelized. Remove from the heat and let cool. Dice the pineapple.

3. Prepare the salsa. In a small bowl, combine the pineapple, jalapeño, onion, cilantro, and lime juice. Taste and season with salt and pepper.

4. Assemble each taco with about ¼ cup lentils and 2 tablespoons salsa. Roll the tacos and serve immediately.

Nutrition per taco
Calories 170 | Total Fat 1g | Saturated Fat 0g | Cholesterol 0mg | Sodium 55mg | Total Carbohydrate 33g | Dietary Fiber 10g | Sugars 5g | Protein 8g

GREEK WHITE BEAN TACOS

This twist on the traditional taco features ingredients typically found in a Greek salad. Romaine lettuce and cucumber add freshness and crunch to the creamy white beans and feta.

MAKES 8 ▪ PREP 25 MINS ▪ COOK 1 HR

2 tbsp olive oil

1 garlic clove, crushed

2 cups cooked navy beans

Zest and juice of 1 large lemon

¼ cup vegetable stock

1 tbsp chopped oregano

Salt and pepper

½ cup plain Greek yogurt

8 small corn or flour tortillas

2½ cups shredded Romaine lettuce

2 cups diced Roma tomatoes

1 cup diced English cucumber

4oz (110g) crumbled feta cheese

1. In a small Dutch oven or pot, heat the oil over medium-low heat. Add the garlic and cook for 1 to 2 minutes or until soft but not browned. Stir in the navy beans, lemon zest and juice, and stock.

2. Bring to a light boil and then reduce the heat to low and cook, covered, for 5 to 6 minutes or until the stock has been absorbed. Stir in the oregano. Taste and season with salt and pepper.

3. Assemble each taco with 1 tablespoon yogurt, ½ cup navy bean mixture, ⅓ cup Romaine, ¼ cup tomato, 2 tablespoons cucumber, and 1 tablespoon feta. Serve immediately.

Nutrition per taco
Calories 210 | Total Fat 8g | Saturated Fat 3g | Cholesterol 15mg | Sodium 190mg | Total Carbohydrate 28g | Dietary Fiber 7g | Sugars 3g | Protein 11g

PINTO BEAN & SPIRALIZED SWEET POTATO QUESADILLA

This quesadilla—a pressed, cheesy Mexican snack—is a great combination of heat from the jalapeño and sweetness from the potato. Spiralizing the sweet potato adds great texture to the dish.

MAKES 4 ▪ PREP 20 MINS ▪ COOK 40 MINS

1 small sweet potato, peeled

2 tbsp vegetable oil

1 jalapeño, deseeded and diced

4 large flour tortillas

2 cups finely shredded sharp Cheddar cheese

1⅓ cups cooked pinto beans

½ cup chopped green onion

½ cup chopped cilantro

Sour cream, to serve

1. With a spiralizer or mandoline, slice the sweet potato into medium strands.

2. In a medium skillet, heat the oil over medium heat until shimmering. Add the jalapeño and cook for 5 minutes or until softened but not browned. Add the sweet potato and cook for 7 minutes or until tender but still al dente.

3. To assemble each quesadilla, sprinkle ¼ cup Cheddar on the lower half of the tortilla. Top the Cheddar with ⅓ cup pinto beans and ⅓ cup sweet potato mixture. Add 2 tablespoons onion and 2 tablespoons cilantro. Top with an additional ¼ cup Cheddar. Fold the tortilla in half. Repeat to make 4 quesadillas total.

4. Heat a nonstick skillet over medium heat. Working one at a time, cook each quesadilla for about 8 minutes, flipping halfway through, until the tortilla is golden brown and the Cheddar is melted.

5. Cut each quesadilla into 4 sections. Serve immediately with sour cream on side.

MAKE IT WITH MEAT Layer 1 ounce (25g) cooked, shredded chicken or pork into each quesadilla before browning.

Nutrition per quesadilla

Calories 640 | Total Fat 33g | Saturated Fat 17g | Cholesterol 75mg | Sodium 840mg | Total Carbohydrate 61g | Dietary Fiber 9g | Sugars 4g | Protein 26g

LENTIL PATE BANH MI

Creamy lentils replace traditional pate in this version of the Vietnamese sandwich. Don't skip the sprouted lentils—the texture of these and the crisp vegetables are delightful.

MAKES 4 ▪ PREP 40 MINS ▪ COOK 10 MINS, PLUS 1 HR TO CHILL

1 cup cooked green lentils

½ cup roughly chopped walnuts

1 tbsp miso paste

1 tsp soy sauce or liquid aminos

2 tsp apple cider vinegar

1½ tbsp olive oil

Salt and pepper

½ cup shredded carrot

½ cup grated daikon

⅓ cup rice wine vinegar

Pinch of granulated sugar

½ cup sprouted brown lentils

1 long, thin French baguette

⅓ cup mayonnaise

1 small cucumber, peeled and cut into long strips

2 small jalapeños, thinly sliced

2 cups cilantro sprigs

1. Make the lentil pate. In a food processor, combine the green lentils, walnuts, miso paste, soy sauce, and apple cider vinegar. Blend on low and drizzle in the oil until smooth. Taste and season with salt and pepper. Transfer to a small bowl and cover with plastic wrap, pressing the plastic onto top of the lentil pate. Refrigerate for 1 hour.

2. In another small bowl, make the pickled carrot mixture by mixing together the carrot, daikon, rice wine vinegar, sugar, and sprouted lentils. Toss to coat thoroughly. Refrigerate, covered, for at least 1 hour.

3. Preheat the oven to 350°F (180°C). Horizontally slice through the baguette, leaving the side intact so the sides are hinged. Cut fully through the baguette to make 4 equal sections. Place the 4 sections open on a rimmed baking sheet and toast for 5 minutes, or until crispy but not hard. Let cool.

4. To assemble the sandwiches, spread equal amounts mayonnaise on the top pieces. Spread equal amounts lentil pate on the bottom pieces. Top the lentil pate with equal amounts pickled carrot mixture, cucumber, jalapeños, and cilantro. Serve immediately.

WHY NOT TRY... To make the banh mi heartier, add 1 ounce (25g) sliced and grilled tofu to each sandwich.

Nutrition per sandwich
Calories 440 | Total Fat 24g | Saturated Fat 6g | Cholesterol 15mg | Sodium 760mg |
Total Carbohydrate 46g | Dietary Fiber 8g | Sugars 10g | Protein 10g

BRAISES & CURRIES

BRAISED LEEKS & LE PUY LENTILS

Simple to make yet sophisticated in flavor, braising leeks brings out their subtle sweetness and contrasts beautifully with the earthy flavor of French Le Puy lentils.

SERVES 6 ▪ PREP 15 MINS ▪ COOK 30 MINS

6 leeks

3 tbsp unsalted butter

1 tbsp dry vermouth

3 thyme sprigs

½ cup vegetable stock

1 cup cooked Le Puy or green lentils

Salt and pepper

2 tbsp chopped flat-leaf parsley

1. Carefully trim and remove the root from the leeks while keeping them intact. Cut off the dark green tops and remove the tough outer layers. Cut each leek in half lengthwise. Submerge the leeks in cold water for 5 minutes to remove any dirt from the layers. Transfer to a colander and let drain.

2. In a 12-inch (30cm) skillet, melt the butter over medium-low heat. Add the vermouth. Place the leeks cut-side down in the skillet and cook for 4 minutes.

3. Add the thyme and stock. Bring to a gentle boil then reduce the heat and simmer, covered, for 10 to 15 minutes or until the leeks are fork tender.

4. Add the lentils and cook for an additional 5 minutes. Taste and season with salt and pepper.

5. Remove the thyme stems. With tongs, transfer the leeks to a serving platter. Pour the lentils and cooking liquid over the leeks. Garnish with parsley and serve immediately.

MAKE IT VEGAN   Replace the butter with a vegan butter alternative.

Nutrition per serving
Calories 150 | Total Fat 6g | Saturated Fat 3g | Cholesterol 15mg | Sodium 20mg |
Total Carbohydrate 19g | Dietary Fiber 4g | Sugars 4g | Protein 4g

CHICKPEA TIKKA MASALA
IN LETTUCE CUPS

Creamy and surprisingly mild, the curry flavor in this dish is a wonderful match for the slightly sweet butter lettuce and the textured chickpeas.

SERVES 6 ▪ PREP 20 MINS ▪ COOK 35 MINS

1 tbsp ghee

1 small yellow onion, diced

1 tbsp garam masala

½ tsp turmeric

1 small green chile, deseeded and minced

¼ tsp grated ginger

2½ cups cooked chickpeas

2 cups tomato purée

¼ cup plain Greek yogurt

Salt and pepper

12 leaves butter lettuce, washed and dried

¼ cup thinly sliced red onion

2 tbsp chopped cilantro

1. In a large skillet, heat the ghee over medium heat until shimmering. Add the yellow onion and cook for 5 to 10 minutes or until softened. Add the garam masala, turmeric, chile, and ginger. Cook for an additional minute to warm the spices.

2. Stir in the chickpeas and tomato purée. Bring to a boil and then reduce the heat to low. Stir in the yogurt and cook for 20 minutes or until the sauce and the chickpeas are completely warmed through. Taste and season with salt and pepper. Remove from the heat and let sit for 5 minutes.

3. To assemble, portion the chickpea mixture evenly into each leaf. Garnish with red onion and cilantro and serve immediately.

WHY NOT TRY... For texture and crunch, use Savoy or Napa cabbage in place of butter lettuce.

Nutrition per serving
Calories 100 | Total Fat 2.5g | Saturated Fat 1g | Cholesterol <5mg | Sodium 100mg | Total Carbohydrate 15g | Dietary Fiber 4g | Sugars 5g | Protein 5g

GREEN CURRY LENTILS & BROCCOLI

The crunch of broccoli complements the creamy curry sauce, and the lentils introduce another layer of texture to this Thai dish. It's perfect over basmati or jasmine rice.

SERVES 8 ▪ PREP 30 MINS ▪ COOK 40 MINS

1 tbsp vegetable oil

1 shallot, minced

1 garlic clove, minced

1 tbsp green curry paste

1 (14fl oz/400 ml) can full-fat unsweetened coconut milk

½ tbsp soy sauce

1 kaffir lime leaf or 1 tbsp fresh lime juice

1 small red bell pepper, deseeded and julienned

3 cups broccoli florets

1 cup cooked green lentils

3.5oz (100g) shiitake mushrooms, sliced

⅔ cup chopped fresh green beans

1 tbsp finely chopped basil

Salt and pepper

1. In a large pot, heat the oil over medium heat until shimmering. Add the shallot and garlic and cook for 5 to 10 minutes or until softened. Add the curry paste and stir to combine. Cook for an additional minute.

2. Stir in the coconut milk, soy sauce, and kaffir lime leaf or lime juice. Simmer for 10 minutes.

3. Add the red bell pepper and cook for an additional 10 minutes, or until the pepper starts to soften.

4. Stir in the broccoli, lentils, mushrooms, green beans, and basil. Cook for an additional 5 to 10 minutes or until the green beans and broccoli are tender and the mushrooms are cooked. Remove the kaffir lime leaf (if using). Taste and season with salt and pepper. Serve immediately.

MAKE IT WITH MEAT Add ½ pound (225g) raw chicken breast, sliced, and cook with the shallots and garlic in step 1.

Nutrition per serving
Calories 150 | Total Fat 11g | Saturated Fat 9g | Cholesterol 0mg | Sodium 200mg |
Total Carbohydrate 11g | Dietary Fiber 4g | Sugars 3g | Protein 4g

RED KIDNEY BEAN CURRY

Meaty kidney beans are simmered in a spicy onion-tomato sauce to create this simple curry. It's a comforting staple in many Indian households and often served with basmati rice.

SERVES 6 ▪ PREP 25 MINS ▪ COOK 30 MINS

2 tbsp vegetable oil

1 medium onion, diced

3 garlic cloves, finely minced

2 tsp grated ginger

1 small green or red chile, deseeded and minced

1½ cups crushed tomatoes

¼ tsp turmeric

1 tbsp ground coriander

1 tbsp ground cumin

1 ½ tsp garam masala

3 cups cooked kidney beans

½ cup vegetable stock

Salt and pepper

¼ cup chopped cilantro

1. In a heavy-bottomed pot or Dutch oven, heat the oil over medium-high heat. Add the onion and cook for 5 minutes or until it softened. Add the garlic, ginger, and chile, and cook for an additional 1 to 2 minutes.

2. Stir in the crushed tomatoes, turmeric, coriander, cumin, and garam masala. Bring the sauce mixture to a boil and then reduce the heat to low. Cook, covered and stirring regularly, for 7 to 8 minutes or until the sauce begins to thicken.

3. Add the kidney beans and stock. Cook for 10 minutes, stirring regularly, until the beans are heated through. Taste and season with salt and pepper. Portion into a serving bowl, garnish with cilantro, and serve immediately.

MAKE IT WITH MEAT Add ½ pound (225g) raw cubed chicken breast to the pot before adding the garlic in step 1.

Nutrition per serving
Calories 180 | Total Fat 4g | Saturated Fat 3g | Cholesterol 0mg | Sodium 170mg |
Total Carbohydrate 28g | Dietary Fiber 9g | Sugars 4g | Protein 9g

CURRIED SQUASH & MUNG BEAN DOPIAZA

The pronounced flavors of both caramelized onion and lightly sautéed onion combine with the creamy coconut to create this dopiaza, a Hindi word meaning "two onions." Serve with rice or naan.

SERVES 6 ▪ PREP 30 MINS ▪ COOK 1 HR 30 MINS

4 cups peeled and cubed butternut squash

2 tbsp vegetable oil, divided

2 medium yellow onions

2 garlic cloves, minced

1 tsp grated ginger

1½ tsp ground cumin

1 tsp ground coriander

2¼ tsp garam masala

1 tsp red pepper flakes

½ tsp turmeric

¼ cup tomato purée

1 (14fl oz/400ml) can full-fat unsweetened coconut milk

3 Roma tomatoes, roughly chopped

1 cup vegetable stock

3 cups cooked mung beans

⅓ cup chopped cilantro

1. Preheat the oven to 375°F (190°C). Toss the cubed squash with 1 tablespoon oil and spread in an even layer on a baking sheet lined with parchment paper. Roast for 15 to 25 minutes or until tender, stirring occasionally.

2. Meanwhile, dice one onion and thinly slice the other onion. Set aside in separate bowls.

3. Caramelize the sliced onion. In a large saucepan, heat the remaining 1 tablespoon oil over medium-low heat until hot. Add the sliced onion and cook until tender, 5 to 10 minutes. Slightly raise the heat and cook the onions until golden brown, 25 to 30 minutes, gently stirring and using a splash of water as needed to release the onions from the pot. Remove the caramelized onions from the pan and set aside.

4. Add the diced onion to the pan and cook for 5 to 10 minutes over medium heat until softened. Add the garlic and ginger and cook for an additional 1 to 2 minutes. Stir in the cumin, coriander, garam masala, red pepper flakes, and turmeric, and cook for 1 minute to heat spices.

5. Stir in the tomato purée, coconut milk, tomatoes, and stock. Bring to a boil and then reduce the heat and simmer for 5 minutes or until the ingredients are incorporated and the tomatoes are tender. Remove from the heat and let cool.

6. With a blender or immersion blender, purée the tomato mixture until smooth. Heat the sauce back up in the pan over medium-low heat. Add the roasted squash and mung beans. Simmer for 15 minutes, covered, or until the sauce slightly thickens. Stir in the caramelized onions. Garnish with the chopped cilantro and serve immediately.

Nutrition per serving
Calories 320 | Total Fat 17g | Saturated Fat 14g | Cholesterol 0mg | Sodium 65mg | Total Carbohydrate 37g | Dietary Fiber 9g | Sugars 8g | Protein 10g

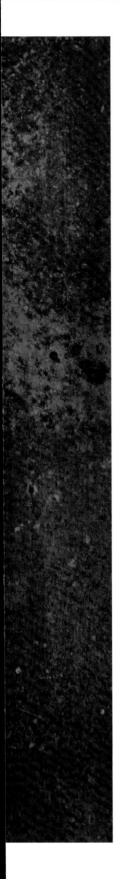

DAL BOLOGNESE

There are few delights more comforting than the flavors of a slow-cooked classic Bolognese sauce, used here to create a warmly spiced lentil dal. This is delicious atop rice or polenta.

SERVES 8 ▪ PREP 30 MINS ▪ COOK 1 HR

2 tbsp olive oil

2 celery stalks, finely diced

1 small yellow onion, finely diced

2 carrots, peeled and finely diced

2 garlic cloves, minced

2 cups dried brown lentils

1 (28oz/794g) can crushed tomatoes

2 tbsp tomato paste

4 cups vegetable stock

1 bay leaf

½ cup heavy cream

¼ tsp ground nutmeg

Salt and pepper

1. In a Dutch oven or heavy-bottomed pot, heat the oil over medium heat until shimmering. Add the celery, onion, and carrot, and cook for 10 minutes or until softened. Add the garlic and cook for another 3 to 4 minutes.

2. Stir in the lentils, crushed tomatoes, tomato paste, stock, and bay leaf. Bring to a gentle boil and then reduce the heat to low and simmer, covered, for 35 minutes or until the lentils are tender and sauce has thickened.

3. Stir in the heavy cream and nutmeg. Cook for an additional 5 minutes. Taste and season with salt and pepper. Remove the bay leaf and serve immediately.

MAKE IT VEGAN Substitute a non-dairy cream or milk.

Nutrition per serving
Calories 290 | Total Fat 10g | Saturated Fat 4g | Cholesterol 20mg | Sodium 180mg | Total Carbohydrate 39g | Dietary Fiber 17g | Sugars 7g | Protein 14g

INDIAN SPICED SPINACH & LENTILS

Inspired by the Indian favorite saag, this recipe incorporates green lentils to add texture to the creamy spinach dish. Serve with warm garlic naan and rice for a complete meal.

SERVES 4 ▪ PREP 15 MINS ▪ COOK 30 MINS

1½ tsp cumin seeds

6 tbsp ghee

1½ tsp turmeric

½ tsp ground coriander

1 large green chile, deseeded and minced

2 garlic cloves, minced

24oz (680g) baby spinach

1½ cups cooked green lentils

¼ cup heavy cream

Salt and pepper

1. With a mortar and pestle, grind the cumin seeds into a fine powder to release fragrance.

2. In a heavy-bottomed pot, heat the ghee over medium heat until shimmering. Add the crushed cumin, turmeric, and coriander and cook for 1 minute. Add the chile and cook for 3 minutes or until it begins to soften. Add the garlic and cook for an additional 2 minutes.

3. Add the spinach. Stir to combine with the spices and aromatics. Cook for 5 minutes or until the spinach begins to wilt.

4. Stir in the green lentils and heavy cream. Bring to a boil and then reduce the heat to low and simmer, partially covered and stirring regularly, for 15 minutes or until the spinach is cooked and the sauce has thickened.

5. Taste and season with salt and pepper. Serve immediately.

MAKE IT VEGAN Replace the ghee with a light vegetable oil and use non-dairy cream.

Nutrition per serving
Calories 420 | Total Fat 11g | Saturated Fat 7g | Cholesterol 10mg | Sodium 135mg |
Total Carbohydrate 57g | Dietary Fiber 32g | Sugars <1g | Protein 24g

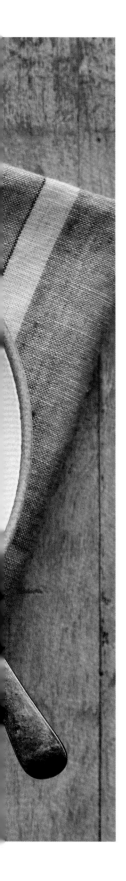

PIGEON PEA VINDALOO

Characteristic of vindaloo, the high heat level in this Indian curry perfectly balances with the warm spices, such as cinnamon and cardamom. Serve with rice or naan and some cooling yogurt.

SERVES 4 ▪ PREP 25 MINS ▪ COOK 40 MINS

1¼ tbsp ground cumin

1 tbsp ground coriander

¾ tsp turmeric

⅔ tsp ground cardamom

½ tbsp ground mustard

1 tbsp paprika

1 tbsp vegetable oil

1 small yellow onion, diced

3 garlic cloves, minced

¾ tbsp minced ginger

1 large Thai chile, deseeded and minced

1 bay leaf

1 cinnamon stick

1 cup tomato purée

1 tbsp red wine vinegar

1 cup water

3 cups cooked pigeon peas

Salt and pepper

1. In a small bowl, combine the cumin, coriander, turmeric, cardamom, mustard, and paprika. Stir thoroughly to combine.

2. In a heavy-bottomed pan, heat the oil over medium heat until shimmering. Add the onion and cook for 5 to 10 minutes or until it starts to become translucent.

3. Stir in the garlic, ginger, and chile, and cook for an additional 2 minutes. Stir in the spice mixture, bay leaf, cinnamon stick, tomato purée, vinegar, and water, Bring to a boil and then reduce the heat and simmer, covered, for 10 minutes.

4. Add the pigeon peas and stir to combine. Bring to a boil and then reduce the heat and simmer, covered, for 20 minutes. Remove the cinnamon stick and bay leaf. Taste and season with salt and pepper. Serve immediately.

MAKE IT WITH MEAT Brown 1 pound (450g) cubed beef chuck and add with the tomato purée.

Nutrition per serving
Calories 250 | Total Fat 5g | Saturated Fat 3g | Cholesterol 0mg | Sodium 590mg |
Total Carbohydrate 42g | Dietary Fiber 12g | Sugars 9g | Protein 11g

MOROCCAN SQUASH & PIGEON PEA TAGINE

This slow-cooked warmly spiced squash stew receives its name from the earthenware pot in which it's traditionally cooked, but you can create the same depth of flavor even without a tagine.

SERVES 6 ▪ PREP 45 MINS ▪ COOK 45 MINS

1 tbsp coconut oil

1 medium yellow onion, chopped

1 carrot, diced

2 garlic cloves, minced

1 tsp grated ginger

1 tsp smoked paprika

1 cinnamon stick

¼ tsp allspice

½ tsp ground coriander

¼ tsp ground cardamom

2 tbsp tomato paste

2 cups vegetable stock

1 large acorn squash, peeled, deseeded, and cubed (about 4 cups)

2 cups cooked pigeon peas

Juice of 1 large lemon

½ cup pitted and chopped dates

Salt and pepper

1. In a cast-iron tagine or large Dutch oven, heat the coconut oil over medium heat until shimmering. Add the onion and carrot and cook for 5 to 10 minutes. Add the garlic and ginger and cook for an additional 1 to 2 minutes.

2. Stir in the paprika, cinnamon stick, allspice, coriander, and cardamom. Cook for 1 minute to warm the spices. Add the tomato paste and stock and stir to combine.

3. Stir in the squash. Bring to a boil over high heat and then reduce the heat and simmer, covered, for 15 minutes. Add the pigeon peas and cook for an additional 10 minutes or until the squash is tender and the peas are warmed through. Stir in the lemon juice and dates. Taste and season with salt and pepper. Remove the cinnamon stick and serve immediately.

MAKE IT WITH MEAT Brown 1 pound (450g) cubed lamb shoulder and add with the acorn squash.

Nutrition per serving
Calories 210 | Total Fat 2.5g | Saturated Fat 2g | Cholesterol 0mg | Sodium 260mg |
Total Carbohydrate 41g | Dietary Fiber 8g | Sugars 22g | Protein 5g

CAJUN BRAISED BLACK-EYED PEAS

Vinegar and spicy cayenne balance earthy black-eyed peas for Southern Creole flavor. Serve these brothy beans with cooked brown rice or quinoa to make a true cajun meal.

SERVES 4 ▪ PREP 15 MINS ▪ COOK 55 MINS

1 tbsp canola or vegetable oil

1 medium green bell pepper, finely diced

1 medium yellow onion, finely diced

1 celery stalk, finely diced

1 garlic clove, minced

5 thyme sprigs

1 bay leaf

2½ cups vegetable stock

2 cups soaked black-eyed peas

¾ tsp cayenne

½ tsp paprika

1 tbsp white wine vinegar

Salt and pepper

1. In a medium Dutch oven or heavy-bottomed pot, heat the oil over medium heat until shimmering. Add the bell pepper, onion, and celery. Cook for 5 to 10 minutes or until softened. Add the garlic and cook for an additional 1 to 2 minutes.

2. Add the thyme, bay leaf, and stock. Bring to a boil and then reduce the heat and simmer for 5 minutes. Stir in the black-eyed peas, cayenne, and paprika.

3. Bring to a boil and then reduce heat to low and simmer, covered, for 30 to 40 minutes or until the peas are tender. Add up to ½ cup additional stock or water as needed.

4. Stir in the vinegar. Taste and season with salt and pepper. Remove the thyme stems and bay leaf. Serve immediately.

MAKE IT WITH MEAT Add 2½ ounces (70g) cooked cubed ham or smoked pork to the braising liquid along with the beans.

Nutrition per serving
Calories 270 | Total Fat 5g | Saturated Fat 0g | Cholesterol 0mg | Sodium 780mg | Total Carbohydrate 41g | Dietary Fiber 11g | Sugars 5g | Protein 13g

SWEET & SOUR CABBAGE
WITH BROWN LENTILS

This is an easy version of a German classic. Sugar, apple, and vinegar combine for a pleasantly smooth flavor that's even more delicious when re-heated the next day.

SERVES 4 ▪ PREP 20 MINS ▪ COOK 50 MINS

1 tbsp olive oil

1 shallot, minced

1 head red cabbage, core removed, shredded

1 small Granny Smith apple, peeled and julienned

¼ tsp fennel seeds

3 tbsp light brown sugar

½ cup apple cider vinegar

1 cup cooked brown lentils

1. In a Dutch oven or heavy-bottomed pot, warm the oil over medium heat until shimmering. Add the shallot and cook for 3 minutes or until softened but not brown. Stir in the cabbage and apple.

2. Add the fennel seeds, brown sugar, and vinegar. Bring to a boil and then reduce the heat to low and simmer, covered, for 25 minutes.

3. Add the lentils, stir thoroughly, and re-cover. Cook for an additional 20 minutes or until the cabbage is tender and the lentils are warmed through. Serve immediately.

Nutrition per serving
Calories 210 | Total Fat 4g | Saturated Fat 0g | Cholesterol 0mg | Sodium 60mg | Total Carbohydrate 41g | Dietary Fiber 9g | Sugars 23g | Protein 8g

BRAISED CHICKPEAS
WITH PRESERVED LEMON

A North African condiment, these lemon slices packed in a brine of salt and water add a fragrant touch to this simple chickpea and chard braise.

SERVES 6 ▪ PREP 15 MINS ▪ COOK 40 MINS

1 tbsp olive oil

1 small yellow onion, chopped

1 garlic clove, minced

3 cups cooked chickpeas

1lb (450g) Swiss chard (chopped leaves and stems)

½ cup vegetable stock

½ cup chopped pitted green olives

½ tbsp minced preserved lemon, or zest and juice of 1 medium lemon

Salt and pepper

1. In a large Dutch oven or heavy-bottomed pot, heat the oil over medium heat until shimmering. Add the onion and cook for 5 to 10 minutes or until softened. Add the garlic and cook for an additional minute.

2. Add the chickpeas and Swiss chard and stir to combine. Add the stock and cook, covered, for 15 minutes or until the chard begins to wilt.

3. Stir in the olives and preserved lemon. Cook, covered, for an additional 10 minutes. Taste and season with salt and pepper. Serve immediately.

Nutrition per serving
Calories 190 | Total Fat 6g | Saturated Fat 1g | Cholesterol 0mg | Sodium 530mg |
Total Carbohydrate 29g | Dietary Fiber 8g | Sugars 7g | Protein 9g

FRIJOLES BORRACHOS

This Mexican recipe translates to "drunken beans"—a savory, soupy, and scrumptious all-purpose dish.

SERVES 8 ▪ PREP 20 MINS, PLUS 8 HRS FOR SOAKING ▪ COOK 1 HR 35 MINS

8 cups vegetable stock, plus more if needed

1lb (450g) dried pinto beans, presoaked for at least 8 hours, rinsed and drained

1 large white onion, halved, divided

3 garlic cloves, divided

1 tbsp vegetable oil

1 small Serrano chile, deseeded and minced

2 large tomatoes, chopped

12oz (354ml) dark Mexican beer

2 tbsp tomato paste

Salt and pepper

1. In a large stockpot, combine the stock, soaked pinto beans, 1 onion half, and 1 garlic clove. Bring to a boil and then reduce the heat to medium and simmer covered, for 45 to 60 minutes or until the beans are tender, adding additional stock as needed.

2. Meanwhile, dice the remaining 1 onion half and mince the remaining 2 garlic cloves.

3. Remove the pot from the heat, drain the beans into a colander, and discard the garlic clove and large onion pieces. Set the beans aside and let continue to drain.

4. Wipe out the pot. Add the oil and return the pot to the stove over medium heat. Cook the diced onion half for 5 to 10 minutes or until softened. Add the minced garlic and chile and cook for an additional minute.

5. Add the pinto beans, tomatoes, beer, and tomato paste. Stir to combine. Simmer, partially covered, for 20 minutes or until the beer cooks off and the liquid thickens slightly. Taste and season with salt and pepper. Serve immediately.

MAKE IT WITH MEAT For a natural smoky addition, cook 2 slices chopped bacon along with onions and garlic in step 4.

Nutrition per serving
Calories 270 | Total Fat 2.5g | Saturated Fat 1.5g | Cholesterol 0mg | Sodium 430mg | Total Carbohydrate 45g | Dietary Fiber 11g | Sugars 6g | Protein 13g

LENTIL & TOMATO BRAISED GREEN BEANS

The secret of this dish is in the yellow tomatoes—they have an acidity that brightens the entire recipe. You'll be surprised at the depth of flavor achieved from such a simple braise.

SERVES 6 ▪ PREP 15 MINS ▪ COOK 1 HR 15 MINS

¾lb (365g) green beans

1 tbsp olive oil

1 small yellow onion, finely diced

1 garlic clove, minced

2 cups (about 475g) golden cherry tomatoes, halved

¼ cup dry white wine

1½ cups vegetable stock

Pinch of red pepper flakes

⅔ cup cooked brown lentils

Salt and pepper

1. Remove the ends from the green beans. Rinse and let drain. In a medium Dutch oven or heavy-bottomed pot, heat the oil over medium heat until shimmering. Add the onion and cook for 5 to 10 minutes or until softened. Add the garlic and cook for an additional minute.

2. Add the cherry tomatoes and dry white wine. Stir to combine and cook, covered, for 5 minutes. Add stock and red pepper flakes. Bring to a boil and then reduce the heat and simmer, covered, for 15 minutes, stirring occasionally.

3. Add the green beans. Return to a simmer and cook, covered, for 10 minutes. Stir in the brown lentils and cook, covered, for 30 minutes or until the green beans are tender and the liquid thickens. Taste and season with salt and pepper.

4. Remove from the heat and let sit, covered, for 5 to 10 minutes to let any remaining liquid thicken. Serve immediately.

MAKE IT WITH MEAT For a salty, smoky flavor, cook 1 ounce (25g) pancetta along with the onion.

Nutrition per serving
Calories 140 | Total Fat 2.5g | Saturated Fat 0g | Cholesterol 0mg | Sodium 40mg |
Total Carbohydrate 21g | Dietary Fiber 9g | Sugars 5g | Protein 7g

BAKES & CASSEROLES

THREE BEAN PAELLA

This colorful twist on the classic Spanish dish features a trio of meaty pulses in addition to saffron-scented rice, roasted red peppers, and briny green olives.

SERVES 10 ▪ PREP 35 MINS ▪ COOK 1 HR 5 MINS

2 tbsp olive oil

1 medium yellow onion, chopped

3 garlic cloves, minced

Pinch of saffron threads

Pinch of red pepper flakes

1 cup crushed tomatoes

1 tsp smoked paprika

2½ cups Bomba or Calisparra rice

3 cups vegetable stock

¾ cup cooked navy beans

¾ cup cooked pigeon peas

¾ cup cooked kidney beans

½ cup frozen green peas, thawed

Salt and pepper

½ cup roasted red pepper strips

½ cup sliced green Spanish olives

1 large lemon, cut into 8 wedges

Flat-leaf parsley, to garnish

1. In a 10-inch (25cm) paella pan or large cast-iron skillet, warm the oil over medium heat until shimmering. Add the onion and cook for 5 minutes or until it starts to soften. Add the garlic and cook for 30 seconds or until fragrant. Incorporate the saffron, red pepper flakes, tomatoes, and paprika. Stir in the rice and cook for 2 to 3 minutes.

2. Stir in the stock. Bring to a boil and then reduce the heat to low and simmer, covered, for 20 minutes. Stir in the navy beans, pigeon peas, and kidney beans. Cover again and cook for an additional 10 minutes. Scatter the green peas across top and cook without stirring, covered, for an additional 10 minutes or until the beans and peas are warmed through and the rice is cooked. Remove from the heat.

3. Taste and season with salt and pepper. Arrange the roasted red pepper strips and olives evenly across the top. Cover and let the paella stand for 5 minutes. Garnish with parsley and serve with lemon wedges.

MAKE IT WITH MEAT Add ½ pound (225g) cooked, peeled and deveined shrimp along with the red pepper strips in step 3.

Nutrition per serving
Calories 290 | Total Fat 4.5g | Saturated Fat 0.5g | Cholesterol 0mg | Sodium 260mg | Total Carbohydrate 55g | Dietary Fiber 6g | Sugars 4g | Protein 8g |

LIMA BEAN ENCHILADAS

Tomatillos are a staple in Mexican sauces. Their tart, fruity flavor shines in this herbaceous enchilada sauce, wonderfully set off by buttery lima beans and a sweet medley of vegetables.

MAKES 10 ▪ PREP 55 MINS ▪ COOK 1 HR

1½lbs (680g) tomatillos, husked and roughly chopped

2 medium jalapeños, deseeded and chopped

1 medium white onion, chopped

1 cup cilantro sprigs

⅔ cup vegetable broth

Salt and pepper

1 tbsp vegetable oil

1 garlic clove, minced

2 medium zucchini, diced

1 cup fresh yellow or white corn kernels

4 cups packed baby spinach

1½ tsp ground cumin

1 tsp ground coriander

Pinch of red pepper flakes

1½ cups cooked lima beans

10 small white corn tortillas

8oz (266g) shredded Monterey Jack or Mozzarella cheese

½ cup chopped cilantro

1. Preheat the oven to 350°F (180°C). On a greased rimmed baking sheet, arrange the tomatillos, jalapeños, and onion. Roast for 20 to 25 minutes or until tender. Let cool slightly. To make the sauce, transfer the roasted vegetables to a blender and combine with cilantro sprigs and broth. Blend until completely smooth. Season with salt and pepper.

2. Make the filling. In a large skillet, heat the oil over medium heat until shimmering. Add the garlic and cook for 1 to 2 minutes or until soft. Add the zucchini and corn and cook, covered, for an additional 2 to 3 minutes or until the zucchini starts to soften. Stir in the spinach, cumin, coriander, and red pepper flakes. Cover and cook for an additional 3 to 4 minutes until the spinach slightly wilts. Stir in the lima beans. Taste and season with salt and pepper. Remove from the heat and let cool slightly.

3. Spray a 9 × 13-inch (23 × 33cm) glass or ceramic baking dish with cooking spray. Lightly coat the bottom with the sauce. Working one at a time to assemble, add 4 tablespoons filling onto the tortilla and top with 1½ to 2 tablespoons Monterey Jack. Roll tightly and place seam-side down in the dish. Repeat to make 10 enchiladas in total.

4. Top the enchiladas with the remaining sauce. Sprinkle the remaining Monterey Jack over the top. Cover with foil and bake for 15 minutes. Uncover and bake for an additional 10 minutes, or until the Monterey Jack melts. Garnish with chopped cilantro and serve immediately.

MAKE IT WITH MEAT Reduce the zucchini to one and add 4½ ounces (130g) cooked, shredded chicken or pork to filling.

WHY NOT TRY... Use crumbled queso fresco instead of shredded cheese.

Nutrition per enchilada
Calories 180 | Total Fat 6g | Saturated Fat 3g | Cholesterol 10mg | Sodium 340mg |
Total Carbohydrate 23g | Dietary Fiber 5g | Sugars 5g | Protein 10g

MEXICAN TAMALE SKILLET PIE

Tamales are a traditional Mexican dish of masa (cornmeal) filled with meat or vegetables. Here, the tamale is the cornbread topping for a skillet of beans and spices.

SERVES 10 ▪ PREP 40 MINS ▪ COOK 50 MINS

1 tbsp olive oil

1 medium yellow onion, diced

1 garlic clove, minced

1 small jalapeño, deseeded and minced

1 medium red bell pepper, deseeded and diced

1 medium zucchini squash, diced

1½ cups yellow corn kernels

1 tsp chipotle chili powder

1 tbsp ground cumin

1 (14oz/411g) can diced tomatoes (undrained)

2 tbsp tomato paste

¾ cup vegetable broth

1½ cups cooked pinto beans

1 cup cooked kidney beans

¾ cup all-purpose flour

¾ cup yellow cornmeal

1 tsp salt

1 tsp granulated sugar

¾ tsp baking powder

¼ tsp baking soda

¾ cup whole milk

1 large egg

3 tbsp unsalted butter, melted

1. Preheat the oven to 425°F (220°C). In a 10-inch (25cm) cast-iron or ovenproof skillet, warm the oil over medium heat until shimmering. Add the onion and cook for 5 to 10 minutes or until softened. Add the garlic and jalapeño and cook for an additional minute.

2. Add the bell pepper, zucchini, and corn. Cook for 2 to 3 minutes. Incorporate the chipotle chili powder and cumin. Pour in the diced tomatoes, tomato paste, broth, pinto beans, and kidney beans. Mix thoroughly. Bring to a boil and then reduce the heat to low and simmer for 8 to 10 minutes. Remove from the heat.

3. Meanwhile, make the cornbread batter. In a large mixing bowl, whisk together the flour, cornmeal, salt, sugar, baking powder, and baking soda. In another small bowl, stir together the milk and egg. Add the milk-egg mixture to the flour mixture. Then drizzle in the melted butter and stir.

4. To assemble, spread the cornbread batter across the top of the skillet mixture. Bake for 15 minutes or until the cornbread is completely baked and lightly golden brown. Serve immediately.

MAKE IT WITH MEAT Brown ½ pound (225g) raw ground beef or turkey along with garlic.

Nutrition per serving
Calories 280 | Total Fat 8g | Saturated Fat 3g | Cholesterol 30mg | Sodium 170mg | Total Carbohydrate 45g | Dietary Fiber 6g | Sugars 5g | Protein 7g

CURRIED BLACK GRAM STUFFED ONIONS

The nuttiness of black gram and quinoa mixed with the creamy goat cheese makes these stuffed onions a unique vegetarian entrée.

MAKES 8 ▪ PREP 30 MINS ▪ COOK 1 HR

4 medium yellow onions

1 cup water

2¼ cups vegetable broth

½ tsp curry powder

½ tsp garam masala

1 cup dried tri-color quinoa

¾ cup cooked black gram

6oz (170g) crumbled goat cheese

¼ cup plus 2 tbsp chopped cilantro, divided

Salt and pepper

1. Preheat the oven to 375°F (190°C). Trim both ends off of the onions and discard the skin. Cut each onion horizontally in half to create 2 flat sections. To create a well for filling, with a spoon or melon baller, gently scoop out the middle of each onion half, leaving the bottom of the onion intact.

2. Arrange the onions in an 8-inch (20cm) square glass or ceramic baking dish, well-side up, and fill the bottom of the dish with the water. Cover the dish with foil and bake for 40 minutes or until the onions are tender.

3. Meanwhile, in a medium saucepan, combine the broth, curry powder, and garam masala. Bring to a gentle boil and add the quinoa. Return to a boil, and then reduce the heat and simmer, covered, for 15 to 18 minutes or until the quinoa is cooked. Remove the from heat and let sit, covered, for 5 minutes.

4. In a large mixing bowl, combine the cooked and seasoned quinoa, black gram, goat cheese, and ¼ cup cilantro. Thoroughly combine. Taste and season with salt and pepper.

5. Spoon an equal amount quinoa mixture into each onion half. Bake, uncovered, for 20 minutes, or until the filling is toasted and warmed through. Garnish with the remaining 2 tablespoons cilantro and serve immediately.

MAKE IT WITH MEAT Reduce the cooked black gram to ½ cup and add ½ pound (225g) cooked ground lamb along with the onion.

Nutrition per onion half
Calories 240 | Total Fat 7g | Saturated Fat 3.5g | Cholesterol 10mg | Sodium 140mg | Total Carbohydrate 30g | Dietary Fiber 6g | Sugars 4g | Protein 12g |

MOTH BEAN STUFFED SWEET POTATOES
WITH BRIE & POMEGRANATE

The surprising mix of sweet and savory in these baked potatoes makes for a truly luscious vegetarian meal or hearty side dish.

MAKES 8 ▪ PREP 15 MINS ▪ COOK 1 HR 15 MINS

4 medium sweet potatoes (about 2lbs/1kg)

2 cups cooked moth beans

8oz (227g) Brie

Salt and pepper

1 cup pomegranate seeds

1 cup roughly chopped cilantro

1. Preheat the oven to 425°F (220°C) and line a baking sheet with aluminum foil.

2. Cut each potato in half lengthwise. Lightly spray each cut side with cooking spray. Arrange the potatoes cut-side down on the baking sheet and bake for 30 to 40 minutes or until fork-tender all the way through.

3. To assemble, turn the sweet potato halves cut-sides up. With a fork, fluff the inside of the sweet potatoes while keeping the skins intact. Top each potato half with ¼ cup moth beans and 1 ounce (28g) Brie. Season with salt and pepper.

4. Bake for an additional 8 to 10 minutes or until the Brie is melted and gooey. Sprinkle each potato half with 2 tablespoons pomegranate seeds and 2 tablespoons chopped cilantro. Serve immediately.

MAKE IT WITH MEAT Crumble 2 ounces (55g) cooked bacon and add equal amounts to each sweet potato along with the pomegranate seeds.

Nutrition per sweet potato half
Calories 320 | Total Fat 9g | Saturated Fat 5g | Cholesterol 30mg | Sodium 210mg | Total Carbohydrate 48g | Dietary Fiber 6g | Sugars 16g | Protein 15g |

GREEK STUFFED TOMATOES

Dill and mint are tasty in stuffed tomatoes. Serve these with the lids on for a fun presentation.

MAKES 6 ▪ PREP 30 MINS ▪ COOK 50 MINS

6 large red tomatoes

¾ cup vegetable stock, divided

3 tbsp olive oil, divided

1 small yellow onion, finely diced

2 garlic cloves, minced

2 tbsp tomato paste

¼ cup chopped dill

¼ cup chopped mint

¼ cup chopped flat-leaf parsley

Zest and juice of 1 lemon

1 cup cooked navy beans

1 cup cooked brown basmati rice

Salt and pepper

1. Preheat the oven to 400°F (200°C). Cut the top quarter off the tomatoes and scoop out the seeds. Reserve the tops. Place the tomatoes in an ungreased baking dish. Pour ½ cup stock into the dish.

2. In a large skillet, heat 1 tablespoon oil over medium heat until shimmering. Add the onion and cook for 5 to 10 minutes or until softened. Add the garlic and cook for 1 minute.

3. Stir in the tomato paste, dill, mint, parsley, lemon zest and juice, remaining ¼ cup stock, navy beans, and rice. Season with salt and pepper to taste.

4. Portion the filling equally into the tomatoes and place tops on. Drizzle with the remaining 2 tablespoons oil. Cover with foil and cook for 20 minutes. Remove the foil and cook for an additional 20 minutes or until tender. Serve immediately.

Nutrition per tomato
Calories 180 | Total Fat 8g | Saturated Fat 1g | Cholesterol 0mg | Sodium 400mg |
Total Carbohydrate 26g | Dietary Fiber 6g | Sugars 7g | Protein 5g |

ASIAN ADZUKI BAKED BEANS

The flavor profile of these baked beans is reminiscent of Korean BBQ—sweet and savory with gentle heat from the Gochujang.

SERVES 8 ▪ PREP 20 MINS ▪ COOK 1 HR 10 MINS

1 tbsp sesame oil

1 medium yellow onion, diced

1 tbsp tomato paste

½ cup firmly packed light brown sugar

2½ tbsp molasses

1½ tsp ground mustard

½ tsp ground ginger

2 tbsp Gochujang

1 tbsp rice wine vinegar

1 tbsp light soy sauce

6 cups cooked adzuki beans

¾ cup vegetable stock

Salt and pepper

1. Preheat the oven to 325°F (180°C). In a large skillet, heat the sesame oil over medium heat until shimmering. Add the onion and cook for 5 to 10 minutes until softened.

2. Add the tomato paste, brown sugar, molasses, mustard, ground ginger, Gochujang, vinegar, and soy sauce. Cook for 2 to 3 minutes or until the mixture bubbles.

3. Add the adzuki beans and stir to combine. Transfer the bean mixture to a 2-quart (2 liter) ungreased baking dish. Pour in the stock and stir gently to mix. Taste and season with salt and pepper.

4. Cover the dish with aluminum foil and cook for 30 minutes. Remove the foil and cook for an additional 20 minutes or until thickened. Serve immediately.

MAKE IT WITH MEAT For a smoky flavor, chop 2 slices raw bacon and cook with the onions in step 1.

Nutrition per serving
Calories 320 | Total Fat 2g | Saturated Fat 0g | Cholesterol 0mg | Sodium 220mg |
Total Carbohydrate 62g | Dietary Fiber 13g | Sugars 20g | Protein 14g

LENTIL & QUINOA STUFFED POBLANOS

These large, mild peppers have a slightly smoky flavor when cooked and hold their shape well, making them excellent for this Tex-Mex stuffing.

SERVES 8 ▪ PREP 20 MINS ▪ COOK 30 MINS

4 poblano peppers

1 tbsp olive oil

1 cup cooked red quinoa

1 cup cooked beluga lentils

1 cup fresh corn kernels

1 tbsp ground cumin

1½ tsp chipotle chili powder

¼ tsp chili powder

½ tsp tomato paste

⅓ cup vegetable broth

½ cup chopped cilantro

8oz (225g) soft goat cheese, divided

1. Preheat the oven to 375°F (190°C). Cut the peppers in half lengthwise, leaving the stems intact, to create two full halves. Remove the seeds. Drizzle with the oil and arrange cut-side down in a 9 × 13-inch (23 × 33cm) glass baking dish. Roast for 10 minutes or until tender but holding shape.

2. Meanwhile, make the stuffing. In a large mixing bowl, combine the quinoa, lentils, corn, cumin, chipotle chili powder, chili powder, tomato paste, broth, cilantro, and 4 ounces (110g) goat cheese.

3. To assemble, fill each roasted pepper half with an equal amount quinoa mixture. Top each with about 1 tablespoon of the remaining goat cheese. Return to the oven and bake for 15 minutes or until warmed through. Serve immediately.

MAKE IT VEGAN Replace the goat cheese with a vegan cream cheese.

MAKE IT WITH MEAT Add 4½ ounces (130g) cooked shredded chicken to the quinoa mixture.

Nutrition per serving
Calories 290 | Total Fat 11g | Saturated Fat 4.5g | Cholesterol 15mg | Sodium 150mg | Total Carbohydrate 38g | Dietary Fiber 7g | Sugars 1g | Protein 14g

CHICKPEA FLOUR SOCCA
WITH HERB & GREEN OLIVE SALAD

Socca—a chickpea flour pancake—hails from the South of France. Its mild, nutty flavor is the perfect canvas for the fresh herbs and flavors of the arugula salad.

MAKES 2 ▪ PREP 5 MINS, PLUS 1 HR FOR BATTER TO REST ▪ COOK 15 MINS

1 cup chickpea flour

1 tsp smoked paprika

Dash of garlic powder

Pinch of salt

3 tbsp olive oil, divided

1 cup water

2 cups arugula

½ cup flat-leaf parsley

¼ cup basil leaves

⅓ cup pitted green olives, halved

Juice of 1 lemon

1. Make the batter. In a medium mixing bowl, add the chickpea flour, paprika, garlic powder, salt, 2 tablespoons oil, and water. Whisk to combine. Let rest at room temperature for 1 hour.

2. With the rack in the middle of the oven, place two 8-inch (20cm) cast-iron or ovenproof skillets in the oven and preheat to 450°F (232°C). (The skillets should heat up with the oven.)

3. When the skillets are heated, carefully remove and swirl 1½ teaspoons oil around in each skillet. Pour half of the batter into each and return to the oven. Bake for 8 minutes. Then turn the broiler on low and cook for an additional 2 minutes. Remove from the oven and let rest for 1 to 2 minutes.

4. Meanwhile, make the herb and olive salad. In a medium bowl, toss together the arugula, parsley, basil, olives, and lemon juice.

5. Place each socca on a serving plate and top with equal amounts salad. Serve immediately.

MAKE IT WITH MEAT For a more filling meal, top the salad with sliced, grilled steak.

Nutrition per socca
Calories 403 | Total Fat 26g | Saturated Fat 3.5g | Cholesterol 0mg | Sodium 237mg |
Total Carbohydrate 32g | Dietary Fiber 7g | Sugars 6g | Protein 12g

BAKED LENTIL SPAGHETTI SQUASH
WITH WALNUTS & GOAT CHEESE

To infuse your diet with complex carbohydrates, spaghetti squash is a healthy alternative to pasta. Each squash half is its own nutty, casserole-type dish in a self-contained serving.

SERVES 2 • PREP 25 MINS • COOK 45 MINS

1 spaghetti squash

2 tbsp olive oil

1½ cups cooked green or Le Puy lentils

½ cup walnuts, toasted and roughly chopped

1 tbsp thyme leaves

Zest of 1 lemon

Salt and pepper

4oz (110g) soft goat cheese

1. Preheat the oven to 375°F (190°C). Cut the spaghetti squash in half lengthwise and use a spoon to scrape out the seeds from each half. Drizzle each half with 1 tablespoon oil and arrange cut-side down on a baking sheet. Cook for 30 to 35 minutes or until tender but not mushy.

2. Meanwhile, in a medium mixing bowl, combine the lentils, walnuts, thyme, and lemon zest. Set aside until the squash is cooked.

3. With a fork, fluff the flesh of the squash to reveal the "spaghetti" strands. Season with salt and pepper to taste. Portion the lentil filling evenly into each half and crumble goat cheese over each. Bake for an additional 10 minutes or until the cheese softens. Serve immediately, directly from squash shell.

MAKE IT WITH MEAT Reduce the lentils to 1 cup and add 4½ ounces (130g) cooked, seasoned ground turkey to the filling.

Nutrition per serving
Calories 700 | Total Fat 46g | Saturated Fat 12g | Cholesterol 25mg | Sodium 610mg | Total Carbohydrate 51g | Dietary Fiber 17g | Sugars 11g | Protein 30g |

PIGEON PEA SAMOSA BAKE

Filled with the unique aromas and flavors of Indian spiced potatoes and pigeon peas, this approachable casserole with a crunchy phyllo top is a nod to traditional samosa pastry.

SERVES 8 ▪ PREP 30 MINS ▪ COOK 50 MINS

4 cups peeled and cubed yukon gold potatoes

1 cup frozen green peas, thawed

3 tbsp ghee, divided

1 small yellow onion, diced

1 small green chile, deseeded and minced

¼ tsp ground ginger

¼ tsp ground coriander

¾ tsp garam masala

1 tsp ground cumin

¼ tsp turmeric

¼ tsp cayenne

¾ tsp curry powder

1 tbsp water

½ cup cooked pigeon peas

⅓ cup vegetable stock

⅓ cup chopped cilantro

Salt and pepper

4 sheets frozen phyllo dough, thawed

1. Preheat the oven to 350°F (180°C). Coat a 9-inch (23cm) round baking dish with cooking spray.

2. Bring a large pot of water to a rolling boil. Add the potatoes and cook for 8 to 10 minutes or until fork-tender. Meanwhile, place the green peas in a fine mesh sieve or colander. When the potatoes are cooked through, pour the potatoes and hot water over peas. Let drain thoroughly.

3. In a 12-inch (31cm) skillet, heat 2 tablespoons ghee over medium heat until shimmering. Add the onion and chile and cook for 5 to 10 minutes or until softened. Stir in the ginger, coriander, garam masala, cumin, turmeric, cayenne, curry powder, and water. Cook for an additional minute until the spices are warmed through.

4. Add the potatoes and green peas, pigeon peas, stock, cilantro, and remaining 1 tablespoon ghee. Stir to combine. Taste and season with salt and pepper. Remove from the heat.

5. Transfer the potato–pigeon pea mixture to the baking dish. Crinkle the phyllo dough and place atop the potato mixture. Bake for 20 to 25 minutes or until the phyllo dough is golden brown. Serve immediately.

MAKE IT WITH MEAT   Add 4½ ounces (130g) cooked, seasoned ground lamb with the peas in step 4.

WHY NOT TRY...   For an aromatic garnish, sprinkle the pastry with crushed cumin seeds before baking.

Nutrition per serving
Calories 150 | Total Fat 4.5g | Saturated Fat 2.5g | Cholesterol 5mg | Sodium 75mg |
Total Carbohydrate 25g | Dietary Fiber 3g | Sugars 2g | Protein 4g

SPICED SWEET POTATO SHEPHERD'S PIE

Sweet potato is a wonderful contrast to the warm spices in this Indian-inspired twist on a classic comfort dish.

SERVES 6 ▪ PREP 35 MINS ▪ COOK 55 MINS

3 medium sweet potatoes

⅓ cup heavy cream

Salt and pepper

2 tbsp ghee

1 medium yellow onion, chopped

1 garlic clove, minced

4 cups cooked brown lentils

1 tbsp ground cumin

1 tbsp garam masala

2 tsp curry powder

1 tsp turmeric

1⅔ cups vegetable stock

½ cup chopped cilantro

½ cup panko breadcrumbs

1. Preheat the oven to 375°F (190°C). In a large pot, bring 6 cups water to a boil. Peel and cube the sweet potatoes. Cook the potatoes for 15 to 20 minutes or until fork-tender. Drain thoroughly and transfer to a large mixing bowl. With a potato masher, mash the potatoes and heavy cream until smooth. Season with salt and pepper to taste.

2. While the potatoes are cooking, in a large skillet, warm the ghee over medium heat. Add the onion and cook for 5 to 10 minutes or until softened. Add the garlic and cook for an additional minute.

3. Add the lentils, cumin, garam masala, curry powder, and turmeric. Stir to combine and cook for 1 to 2 minutes to warm the spices. Add the stock and cook for 5 minutes. Stir in the cilantro.

4. Pour the lentil mixture evenly into a 9 x 3-inch (23 × 33cm) ungreased baking dish. Top with the mashed sweet potato. Bake for 15 minutes. Sprinkle evenly with the breadcrumbs and bake for an additional 10 minutes or until lightly browned. Cool for 10 minutes before serving.

MAKE IT WITH MEAT Add 1 pound (450g) raw ground lamb. Reduce the lentils by half and brown the lamb along with the onions.

Nutrition per serving
Calories 310 | Total Fat 8g | Saturated Fat 4g | Cholesterol 20mg | Sodium 90mg |
Total Carbohydrate 47g | Dietary Fiber 13g | Sugars 7g | Protein 14g |

KIDNEY BEAN CASSOULET

The flaky breadcrumb topping contrasts with the buttery kidney beans in this hearty and textured entrée.

SERVES 4 ▪ PREP 20 MINS ▪ COOK 1 HR

2 tbsp olive oil

1 small yellow onion, diced

1 carrot, diced

1 celery stalk, diced

2 garlic cloves, minced

3 thyme sprigs

1 bay leaf

Pinch of red pepper flakes

3½ cups cooked kidney beans

¾ cup tomato purée

¾ cup vegetable stock

Salt and pepper

⅔ cup panko breadcrumbs

1 tbsp chopped flat-leaf parsley

1. Preheat the oven to 400°F (200°C). Lightly spray a 2-quart (2 liter) baking dish with cooking spray.

2. In a stockpot or Dutch oven, heat the oil over medium heat until shimmering. Add the onion, carrot, and celery, and cook for 5 to 10 minutes or until softened. Add the garlic and cook for an additional minute.

3. Incorporate the thyme, bay leaf, red pepper flakes, kidney beans, tomato purée, and stock. Simmer, covered, for 20 minutes.

4. Remove the bay leaf and thyme stems. In a blender or food processor, purée ½ cup bean mixture until smooth. Return the puréed mixture to the pot and stir to combine. Taste and season with salt and pepper. Transfer the bean mixture to the baking dish.

5. To make the topping, in a small bowl, combine the breadcrumbs and parsley. Top the dish evenly with breadcrumb mixture. Bake for 20 minutes or until the topping is golden brown. Serve immediately.

Nutrition per serving
Calories 330 | Total Fat 8g | Saturated Fat 1g | Cholesterol 0mg | Sodium 95mg | Total Carbohydrate 51g | Dietary Fiber 14g | Sugars 5g | Protein 16g |

DESSERTS

FLOURLESS BLACK BEAN BROWNIES

These brownies are not like any flourless baked good you've tried—they're light, moist, and cakey.

MAKES 12 ▪ PREP 15 MINS ▪ COOK 1 HR

2 cups cooked black beans

½ cup agave nectar

¼ cup coconut oil

1 tsp vanilla extract

Zest of 1 medium orange

¼ tsp salt

½ tsp baking powder

⅓ cup granulated sugar

½ cup unsweetened cocoa powder

3 large eggs, beaten

½ cup semi-sweet chocolate chips

1. Preheat the oven to 350°F (180°C). Lightly spray an 11 x 7-inch (28 x 18cm) metal baking pan with cooking spray. In a food processor, combine the black beans, agave, coconut oil, vanilla, and orange zest until smooth.

2. In a large mixing bowl, combine the salt, baking powder, sugar, and cocoa powder. Incorporate the black bean mixture and eggs.

3. Gently fold in the chocolate chips, being careful not to over-mix the batter.

4. Scrape the batter into the baking pan. Bake for 30 to 35 minutes or until the brownies pull away from the pan and a toothpick inserted into the center comes out clean. Let cool for 15 to 20 minutes before cutting and serving.

MAKE IT VEGAN Replace the eggs with 1 cup unsweetened applesauce.

Nutrition per brownie
Calories 170 | Total Fat 10g | Saturated Fat 7g | Cholesterol 45mg | Sodium 65mg |
Total Carbohydrate 18g | Dietary Fiber 5g | Sugars 7g | Protein 5g |

LENTIL BAKLAVA

There's nothing like baklava—a sticky, rich treat of flaky phyllo pastry, nuts, and honey. Brown lentils add nutritional value to this decadent dessert.

MAKES 24 ▪ PREP 1 HR ▪ COOK 1 HR

1 cup granulated sugar, divided

⅓ cup honey

¾ cup water

3 thyme sprigs

Juice and peel of 1 large orange

2 cups chopped pistachios

2 cups chopped walnuts

2 cups cooked brown lentils

1½ tsp ground cinnamon

¾ tsp ground cardamom

Pinch of salt

1½ sticks (12 tbsp) unsalted butter, melted

1 (16oz/454g) pkg frozen phyllo dough, thawed

1. Make the syrup. In a small saucepan, combine ¼ cup sugar, honey, and water. Bring to a low boil, stirring occasionally, until the sugar has dissolved. Add the thyme, orange juice, and orange peel. Cook over medium-low heat for 10 minutes until slightly thickened. Remove the peel and thyme stems. Remove from the heat and let cool.

2. Meanwhile, in a large bowl, combine the pistachios, walnuts, lentils, cinnamon, cardamom, remaining ¾ cup sugar, and salt.

3. Preheat the oven to 350°F (175°C). Prepare a clean, flat workspace. Brush the bottom and sides of a 9 x 13-inch (23 x 33cm) metal baking pan with melted butter. Trim the phyllo dough to the size of the pan and cover the phyllo dough with a lightly damp cloth to prevent drying as you work.

4. Place 8 phyllo sheets into the bottom of the pan, brushing every other layer with butter. Spread about ⅓ nut mixture on top of layer and distribute evenly. Repeat this process twice to form 3 nut layers total.

5. Top the pastry with 8 more sheets phyllo dough, and generously brush the top layer with melted butter. Score through the layers of pastry with a sharp knife, making 24 square or diamond shaped pieces (cut about three-quarters through while leaving bottom intact).

6. Bake for 40 to 45 minutes or until golden-brown. Let cool for 5 minutes. Cut through scored pieces to the bottom of the pan. Spoon the cooled syrup over the pieces. Let cool completely. Refrigerate, covered, for at least 3 hours to overnight before serving. Store for up to 3 days in an airtight container in the refrigerator.

Nutrition per piece
Calories 260 | Total Fat 16g | Saturated Fat 6g | Cholesterol 20mg | Sodium 125mg |
Total Carbohydrate 26g | Dietary Fiber 3g | Sugars 13g | Protein 5g

ADZUKI BEAN CHOCOLATE PUDDING

A little goes a long way—this chocolate pudding is rich, decadent, and nutty with a smooth texture. The pudding is a perfect match for a garnish of whipped cream and fresh raspberries.

SERVES 6 ▪ PREP 10 MINS, PLUS OVERNIGHT TO SET ▪ COOK 20 MINS

3 tbsp cornstarch

2 tbsp plus ⅓ cup water, divided

1 cup cooked adzuki beans

1 cup unsweetened almond milk, divided

2 tsp vanilla bean paste

¼ cup agave nectar

½ cup unsweetened cocoa powder

6 raspberries, to garnish

1. In a small bowl, whisk together the cornstarch and 2 tablespoons water. Set aside.

2. In a blender, purée the adzuki beans with the remaining ⅓ cup water and ½ cup almond milk until smooth.

3. In a small saucepan, whisk together the remaining ½ cup almond milk, vanilla bean paste, agave, cocoa powder, and puréed adzuki beans until completely smooth.

4. Whisk in the cornstarch mixture and heat over low heat for 8 to 10 minutes until the mixture comes to a low simmer, stirring occasionally to keep smooth. Remove from the heat and let sit at room temperature for 10 minutes.

5. Portion evenly among 6 serving cups, cover each with plastic wrap, and refrigerate overnight to set. Top each serving with a raspberry before serving.

Nutrition per serving
Calories 110 | Total Fat 1.5g | Saturated Fat 0.5g | Cholesterol 0mg | Sodium 35mg | Total Carbohydrate 24g | Dietary Fiber 5g | Sugars 10g | Protein 4g

CRANBERRY PISTACHIO BISCOTTI

Biscotti are Italian cookies that have a two-step baking process. They're wonderfully textured here with chewy cranberries and crunchy pistachios. Enjoy with coffee or tea for a lightly sweet treat.

MAKES 12 ▪ PREP 25 MINS ▪ COOK 1 HR 20 MINS

1¾ cups chickpea flour

1 tsp baking powder

¼ cup coconut oil, slightly warmed

¾ cup granulated sugar

2 tsp vanilla extract

2 large eggs

Zest of 1 large orange

Pinch of ground nutmeg

½ cup dried cranberries

¾ cup coarsely chopped pistachios

1. Preheat the oven to 300°F (150°C). Line a rimmed baking sheet with parchment paper. In a large mixing bowl, combine the chickpea flour and baking powder.

2. In a medium mixing bowl, whisk together the coconut oil, sugar, vanilla, eggs, orange zest, and nutmeg.

3. Make the batter. In the large mixing bowl, fold the oil-sugar mixture into the flour mixture until incorporated. Gently stir in the cranberries and pistachios until just incorporated.

4. Transfer the batter to the sheet and form into a flat rectangular loaf about 1-inch (3cm) tall. Bake for 35 minutes or until lightly browned and set through the center. Let cool for 15 to 20 minutes.

5. Transfer the parchment paper to a flat work surface. Cut the loaf into 12 equal strips. Transfer the parchment paper back to the baking sheet. Flip the strips onto their cut sides and evenly space them on the sheet. Bake again for 20 minutes or until firm and lightly golden brown. Let cool completely before serving or store in an airtight container in the refrigerator for 2 to 3 days.

WHY NOT TRY... Use an equal amount almond extract and chopped almonds rather than vanilla and pistachios.

Nutrition per cookie
Calories 180 | Total Fat 7g | Saturated Fat 4.5g | Cholesterol 30mg | Sodium 20mg |
Total Carbohydrate 25g | Dietary Fiber 2g | Sugars 17g | Protein 4g |

CHICKPEA & PEANUT COOKIES

These cookies have the nutritional boost of chickpeas, plus they only use 6 ingredients and are easy to make.

MAKES 20 ▪ PREP 45 MINS ▪ COOK 15 MINS

1 cup cooked chickpeas
½ cup creamy peanut butter
1 large egg, lightly beaten
1 tsp vanilla extract
½ cup granulated sugar
¾ tbsp agave nectar

1. Preheat the oven to 350°F (180°C). In a food processor, pulse the chickpeas until the consistency of coarse almond meal. Transfer to a medium mixing bowl.

2. Incorporate the peanut butter, egg, vanilla, sugar, and agave. Stir to combine. Refrigerate for 30 minutes.

3. Line a baking sheet with parchment paper. Portion out 1 tablespoon batter, roll into a ball, and place on the sheet. Repeat to use all of the batter. With a spatula, flatten the dough into rounds.

4. Bake the cookies for 7 minutes, and then rotate the sheet 180 degrees and bake for an additional 7 to 8 minutes or until set and lightly golden brown. Let cool to room temperature before removing from the baking sheet. Store in an airtight container on the counter for up to 2 days.

Nutrition per cookie
Calories 80 | Total Fat 3.5g | Saturated Fat 1g | Cholesterol 10mg | Sodium 5mg |
Total Carbohydrate 9g | Dietary Fiber 1g | Sugars 7g | Protein 3g

STRAWBERRY & GREEN LENTIL CRISP

In this recipe, the natural sweetness of the strawberries pairs well with the caramelized topping. Crisps are a great way to use leftover fruit, so you can substitute any kind you have on hand.

SERVES 6 ▪ PREP 30 MINS ▪ COOK 1 HR 10 MINS

1 cup cooked green lentils

1½lbs (680g) strawberries, hulled and quartered

2 tbsp light brown sugar

3 tsp vanilla extract

1 tbsp cornstarch

¾ cup whole wheat flour

¾ cup coarsely chopped almonds

⅓ cup rolled oats

⅓ cup granulated sugar

1½ tsp ground cinnamon

½ cup unsalted butter, melted

1. Preheat the oven to 350°F (180°C). Spread the lentils in an even layer on a rimmed baking sheet. Toast for 20 minutes or until dry and crispy.

2. In an 8-inch (20cm) ungreased baking dish, combine the strawberries, brown sugar, vanilla, and cornstarch. Spread in an even layer.

3. To make the crisp topping, in a separate large mixing bowl, combine the lentils, whole wheat flour, almonds, oats, sugar, and cinnamon. Drizzle in the melted butter and gently combine. Dollop the topping across the top of the strawberry mixture.

4. Bake, uncovered, for 40 minutes or until the strawberry mixture bubbles and the topping is browned. Let cool for 15 to 20 minutes before serving.

Nutrition per serving

Calories 450 | Total Fat 23g | Saturated Fat 10g | Cholesterol 40mg | Sodium 0mg |
Total Carbohydrate 54g | Dietary Fiber 9g | Sugars 25g | Protein 9g |

WHITE BEAN CREPES
WITH APRICOT SAUCE

Crepes are an easy dessert sure to impress. The tartness of the apricot sauce brightens the nutty white bean crepes.

MAKES 12 ▪ PREP 30 MINS ▪ COOK 50 MINS

½lb (225g) fresh apricots, pitted and roughly chopped

2 tbsp plus 2 tsp honey

Juice of 1 medium orange

½ tsp vanilla bean paste

½ tbsp orange marmalade

¼ cup water

1 cup white bean flour

2½ tbsp granulated sugar

1 tsp ground cinnamon

2 tbsp vegetable oil

½ cup water

1 cup unsweetened almond milk

2 tbsp vanilla extract

2 large eggs

Zest of 1 large orange

½ cup chopped hazelnuts or almonds, toasted

Toasted coconut, to garnish

1. Make the apricot sauce. In a medium saucepan, combine the apricots, honey, orange juice, vanilla bean paste, orange marmalade, and water. Bring to a boil and then reduce the heat and simmer, covered, for 20 minutes, stirring occasionally. With a blender or immersion blender, purée until smooth. Set aside.

2. Make the crepe batter. In a large mixing bowl, combine the white bean flour, sugar, and cinnamon. In a separate medium mixing bowl, whisk together the oil, water, almond milk, vanilla, eggs, and orange zest. Pour the almond milk mixture into the flour mixture and stir until combined and smooth.

3. Heat a crepe pan or a 6-inch (15cm) nonstick skillet over medium heat. Pour in ¼ cup batter and gently swirl around the bottom of the pan. Cook for 1 to 2 minutes or until set and pulling away from the sides. Gently flip and cook for an additional 1 to 2 minutes. Repeat to make 12 crepes total.

4. To serve, roll or fold the crepes, drizzle with the apricot sauce, and sprinkle with toasted hazelnuts and coconut on top.

Nutrition per crepe
Calories 130 | Total Fat 5g | Saturated Fat 2g | Cholesterol 30mg | Sodium 25mg | Total Carbohydrate 25g | Dietary Fiber 4g | Sugars 10g | Protein 4g

BERRY & LIME MUNG BEAN POPS

Refreshingly tart and naturally sweet, these pops are the perfect low-calorie treat for a hot day.

MAKES 10 ▪ PREP 20 MINS, PLUS 6 HRS TO FREEZE

1½ cups blueberries

2 cups blackberries

⅓ cup cooked mung beans

3 tbsp lime juice

⅓ cup agave nectar

⅓ cup water

1. In a blender or food processor, purée the blueberries, blackberries, mung beans, lime juice, agave, and water until smooth.

2. Pour the mixture through a fine mesh sieve to remove the seeds. Press the mixture against the sieve to retain as much liquid as possible.

3. Pour the liquid into 10 pop molds. Insert wooden pop sticks into each mold. Freeze for at least 6 hours or overnight before serving.

Nutrition per pop
Calories 45 | Total Fat 0g | Saturated Fat 0g | Cholesterol 0mg | Sodium 0mg |
Total Carbohydrate 11g | Dietary Fiber 2g | Sugars 7g | Protein 1g |

INDEX

ACKNOWLEDGMENTS

ABOUT THE AUTHOR

Tami Hardeman is a professional food stylist for both print and video. Her work is found in countless magazines, cookbooks, and advertisements. She is also a recipe developer and the author behind the internationally recognized food blog *Running with Tweezers*. Tami's recipes and photos have been featured by *CNN*, *The Huffington Post*, *Saveur*, and many more.

THANKS

I would like to thank Alexandra Andrzejewski and the entire team at DK Alpha for their confidence, patience, and guidance. I cannot express my gratitude and love enough to Helene Dujardin, Rachael Daylong, and Abby Gaskins for making these lovely photos come to life. Much appreciation to my family and friends for being my constant cheerleaders. Nothing would be possible—my life, my career, or this book—without the unwavering love, care, and support of my husband, Mike Boutté. I love you, Boop. This book is dedicated to Philis.